CAL...
Science

Interactive Text

Mc Graw Hill **Macmillan McGraw-Hill**

Contents

CHAPTER 1

Living Things Need Energy

Vocabulary

photosynthesis the way plants use sunlight to make food

environment everything that surrounds a living thing

food chain the path of energy in the form of food going from one living thing to another

producer any living thing that makes, or produces, its own food

consumer a living thing that eats other living things

decomposer a living thing that breaks down dead plants and animals

herbivore an animal that eats mostly plants

carnivore an animal that eats other animals

How do living things get energy to live and grow?

omnivore an animal that eats both plants and animals

food web a way of showing how food chains in any place are linked together

compete to try to get the same thing that others need or want

microorganism any kind of living thing that is too small to be seen with just our eyes

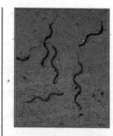

bacteria any of the smallest kinds of microorganism

protist a kind of microorganism larger than bacteria

fungus a plantlike living thing that breaks down dead plants and animals

What are plants?

Plants are living things. They are important for life on Earth. For example, plants make food. The food we eat all starts out from plants. Plants also make *oxygen* (OK•suh•juhn). Oxygen is a gas we breathe. Plants give off oxygen into the air.

Plants come in many shapes, sizes and colors. For example, trees, grasses, and bushes are different kinds of plants. However, most plants have three parts. They have roots, stems, and leaves.

 Quick Check

1. What do plants make?

_____

2. What are three parts that most plants

share? _____

_____

> Leaves collect light from the Sun. They use the light to make food.

> Stems hold a plant up. Water and other materials move through a stem. They may go up to the leaves or down to the roots.

> Roots hold a plant to the ground. They take in water and minerals from the soil.

Here are some plants that hold world records. Some of them are natives of Calfornia.

bamboo

Bamboo plants are the fastest growing plants. Some bamboo plants grow more than 2 centimeters (about 1 inch) an hour.

redwoods

bristlecone pines

Redwoods are the world's tallest plants. They grow in California. Some are over 100 meters (327 feet) tall. Some are over 2,000 years old.

The oldest trees are the bristlecone pines. They live in California's White Mountains. One bristlecone pine is almost 5,000 years old.

✅ Quick Check

3. Which of these amazing plants live in California? Why are they

amazing? _____

_____

How do plants get energy?

Most plants carry out photosynthesis (foh•toh•SIN•thuh•suhs). **Photosynthesis** is the way plants make their own food. To make food, plants need:

• sunlight
• water
• a gas (carbon dioxide)

The food plants make is sugar. The sugar has energy in it. Plants need the energy to live and grow. When we eat plants, we get that energy.

Getting Sunlight

Plants look green because they contain a green material, chlorophyll (KLAWR•uh•fil). Chlorophyll traps sunlight, energy from the Sun. A plant uses the energy to make sugar. The sugar is made in their leaves.

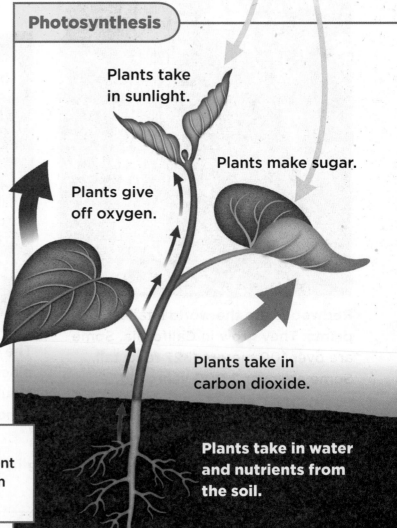

Photosynthesis

Plants take in sunlight.

Plants make sugar.

Plants give off oxygen.

Plants take in carbon dioxide.

Plants take in water and nutrients from the soil.

Reading Diagrams

Follow the arrows to see how a plant takes in sunlight, water, and carbon dioxide and give off oxygen.

Getting Water and Carbon Dioxide

Plants get water from the ground. Most plants you know have roots to take in water. Once inside the roots, water travels up through thin tubes:

- from the roots, water goes up the stem
- from the stem, water goes into leaves

Carbon dioxide is a gas in the air. Plants have tiny holes to take in this gas. These holes are the stomata (STOH•muh•tuh). They are on the bottom of each leaf. Carbon dioxide enters a leaf through the stomata.

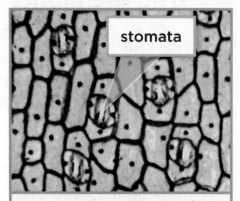

stomata

This photo shows the bottom of a leaf up close. The leaf here is shown over 100 times larger than it really is.

 Quick Check

Write the letter of the word that fits each statement.

4. _____ Plants get this from the Sun.   **a.** chlorophyll

5. _____ Plants make this food.   **b.** energy

6. _____ A green material in plants   **c.** sugar

How are roots and leaves alike? How are they different?

Roots (different)   **Alike**   **Leaves** (different)

7. _____   **8.** _____   **9.** _____

_____

_____

_____

Why are plants important?

Remember, the energy for living things comes from the Sun. Plants can trap this energy. Plants use this energy to make food and oxygen. Food and oxygen are important to animals.

Animals depend on plants for food.

Food

Animals need energy to live. They get energy from food. Animals cannot make their own food. They eat food that comes from plants. Here's how:

How Food Is Passed	Example
Plants make their own food.	A leaf makes food.
Some animals eat plants for food.	A grasshopper eats the leaf.
Some animals eat the animals that eat plants.	A bird eats the grasshopper.

With the food, energy goes from plant to animal to animal.

✔ Quick Check

Label each *True* or *False*. If it is false, correct it.

10. Animals can make their own food. _____

_____

11. Animals need energy to live. _____

_____

This environment is a rain forest.
It is crowded with plants.

Oxygen

Plants make oxygen for themselves and other living things. Animals need oxygen, but cannot make it. Most animals cannot live without oxygen for more than just a few minutes.

Plants Everywhere

Plants live in environments all over Earth. An **environment** is everything that surrounds a living thing. Plants live in all kinds of environments from deserts to oceans. Plants provide energy in food for the living things around them.

✓ Quick Check

Complete this sentence.

12. Animals need plants because _____

_____

LOG ON e-Review Summaries and quizzes online @ www.macmillanmh.com

What is a food chain?

Living things get energy from food. A **food chain** is the path energy takes in the form of food going from one living thing to another.

Here's the path of a food chain:

- The chain starts with energy from the Sun. A plant uses the energy to make its own food. The plant in a food chain is a **producer** because it makes, or produces, its own food.
- Next, an animal such as an insect eats the plant. Energy from the plant passes to the insect. Then another animal, such as a bird, eats that insect. So energy passes from the insect to the bird.

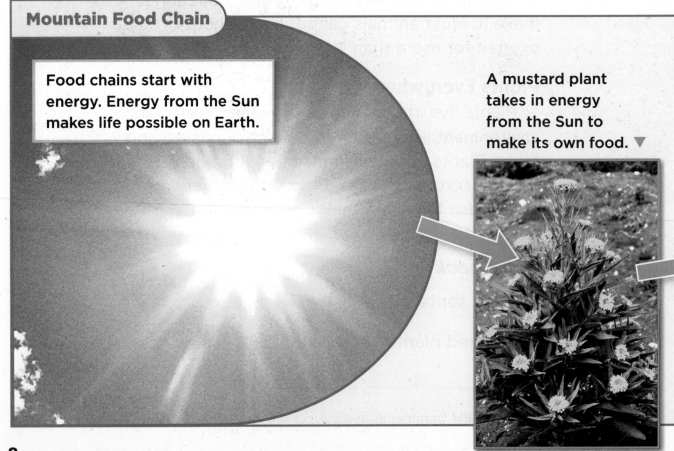

Mountain Food Chain

Food chains start with energy. Energy from the Sun makes life possible on Earth.

A mustard plant takes in energy from the Sun to make its own food. ▼

The insect and the bird are consumers. An animal is a **consumer** because it must eat, or consume, plants or other animals for food.

- Another consumer, such as a wolf, may eat the bird. The chain continues until consumers die.

- At the end of the chain are decomposers. **Decomposers** are tiny living things that break down dead plants and animals. That is, they make dead plants and animals rot. Then they return materials from the dead plants and animals to the soil. Worms and many insects are examples of decomposers.

 Quick Check

Show the order of living things in a food chain.

Producers

↓

13. _____

↓

14. _____

Reading Diagrams

Arrows show the path of energy from the Sun to each living thing in the food chain.

▲ A gopher eats the mustard plant.

A weasel eats the gopher. ▶

A mountain lion eats the weasel. ▶

When the mountain lion dies, decomposers break down its body. ▶

What are herbivores?

In a food chain, the first consumer is an animal that eats a plant. For example, a gopher is a plant eater. A gopher is a herbivore (HUR•buh•vawr). A **herbivore** is an animal that eats mostly plants.

Deer, rabbits, grasshoppers, squirrels, and cows are herbivores. Herbivores are food for other animals. The word for an animal that is hunted by another animal for food is *prey*. All the animals here are prey for some larger or stronger animal.

▲ Herbivores can be as small as this caterpillar.

▲ Antelopes are herbivores. They are also prey to many other animals, such as lions.

◀ The African elephant is Earth's largest land animal. It is a herbivore that eats mostly grasses. It eats from 100 to 200 kilograms (220 to 440 pounds) a day.

✔ Quick Check

15. How do herbivores get energy? _____

_____

_____

What are carnivores and omnivores?

Lions and hawks eat other animals. They are carnivores. A **carnivore** (KAR•nuh•vawr) is an animal that eats other animals.

Some animals eat plants and animals. For example, a bear eats berries, leaves, mice, and squirrels. A bear is an omnivore (AHM•nuh•vawr). An **omnivore** is an animal that eats plants and animals. Raccoons and wasps are omnivores. People are omnivores.

Some animals hunt the animals they eat. Animals that hunt other animals for food are *predators*.

▲ A bear is an omnivore.

▲ A heron is a carnivore.

✔ Quick Check

Write the letter of the food for each kind of animal.

16. _____ herbivore   **a.** mostly animals

17. _____ carnivore   **b.** plants and animals

18. _____ omnivore   **c.** mostly plants

 e-Review Summaries and quizzes online @ www.macmillanmh.com

What are decomposers?

Decomposers are living things at the end of a food chain. They break down plants and animals that have died. The once-living material becomes part of the soil. This material helps other plants to grow. Then food chains can start all over.

There are many kinds of decomposers. Earthworms are decomposers. Insects, such as flies and beetles, are decomposers.

This beetle feeds off things that were once alive. The beetle breaks down "once-living" things.

These earthworms are eating dead plants. They pass materials from the dead plants to the soil. ▶

✔ Quick Check

19. What job do decomposers have in a food chain?

_____

_____

More Food Chains

Here is a food chain in a pond. The producers in this pond are *algae* (AL•jee). Algae are living things that look like tiny plants. They float at the top of a pond or stream or ocean.

Follow the food chain:

1. Sunlight is trapped by algae. Algae make food.

2. Algae are eaten by mayflies.

3. Mayflies are eaten by sunfish.

4. Sunfish are eaten by herons.

5. Decomposers breakdown the herons when they die.

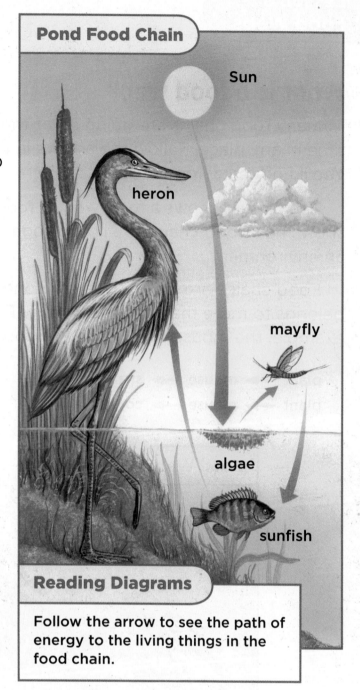

Pond Food Chain

Sun

heron

mayfly

algae

sunfish

Reading Diagrams

Follow the arrow to see the path of energy to the living things in the food chain.

✔ Quick Check

Fill in the blanks to show the path of energy in the pond food chain.

The Sun ➔ **20.** _____ ➔ mayfly ➔ **21.** _____ ➔

22. _____ ➔ decomposers

 e-Review Summaries and quizzes online @ **www.macmillanmh.com**

What is a food web?

Many food chains are going on at the same time in any place. Follow the arrows in the picture. You'll find many food chains.

The picture shows a food web. A **food web** shows how food chains are linked together in an environment.

Food chains are linked when any one animal belongs to more than one food chain. For example, the mouse belongs to two food chains:

plant ➝ mouse ➝ snake

plant ➝ mouse ➝ coyote

Food Web

Food chains show how different living things compete. When living things **compete**, they try to get the same thing, such as food. For example:

• both snakes and coyotes eat mice
• both mice and rabbits eat grass.

✔ *Quick Check*

23. Two animals that the hawk eats are _____

and _____.

24. Two animals that can eat the mouse

are _____ and _____.

Reading Diagrams

The arrows show the path of energy. For example, energy from a leaf goes to the small bird when the bird eats the leaf. The hawk gets energy when the it eats the small bird.

How can food webs change?

Look at the kelp forest food web. Try to find as many food chains as you can. Start with the kelp in the lower left corner. Kelp is a kind of seaweed. Kelp grows in underwater forests. Many kinds of living things eat the kelp.

For example, here are just three food chains. They all start with kelp:

1. kelp ⟶ sea urchins ⟶ sea otters
2. kelp ⟶ sea cucumbers ⟶ crabs ⟶ sea otters
3. kelp ⟶ mussels ⟶ crabs ⟶ sea otters

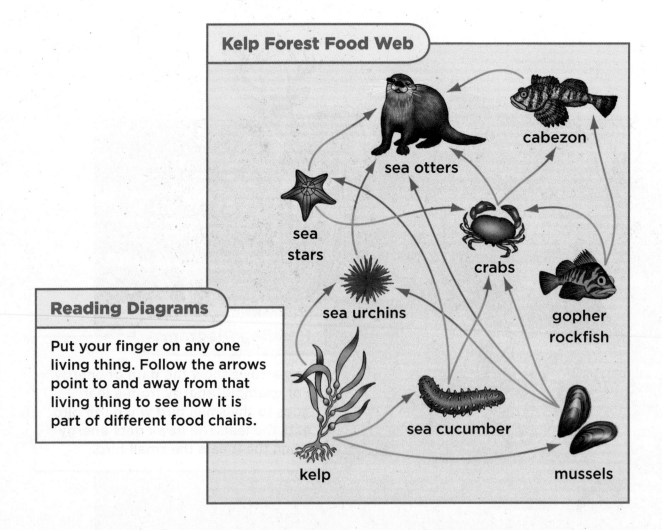

Kelp Forest Food Web

cabezon

sea otters

sea stars

crabs

sea urchins

gopher rockfish

sea cucumber

kelp

mussels

Reading Diagrams

Put your finger on any one living thing. Follow the arrows point to and away from that living thing to see how it is part of different food chains.

Living Things Need Energy

A change in one kind of living thing in a food web causes other kinds of living things to change. For example, over 200 years ago, sea otters were hunted for their fur. So there were fewer and fewer sea otters in the food web.

Look at the kelp forest food web. Sea otters eat sea urchins. Without sea otters, fewer sea urchins were being eaten.

kelp ➞ sea urchins ➞ sea otters

Soon there were too many sea urchins in the kelp forest. They were eating up the kelp. Other living things, such as mussels, could not get the kelp they needed. The mussels began to die out. Then crabs, which eat mussels, began to die out as well.

Many ocean animals eat kelp.

✔ *Quick Check*

Complete these food chains. Use the kelp forest food web on p. 16.

kelp ➞ mussels ➞ **23.** _____ ➞ sea otters

kelp ➞ sea cucumbers ➞ sea stars ➞ **24.** _____

How do new organisms change food webs?

A food web can change when a living thing is added to a place. For example, in Australia, over 70 years ago, insects were eating sugar cane plants. Farmers brought in large toads to eat the insects and save the sugar cane.

The farmers hoped that lizards and birds would eat the some of the toads. They wanted to keep the number of toads from growing.

However, the toads did not eat the insects. They ate the birds and lizards instead! The toads grew in number. They ate just about everything they could, even pets. What's more, the insects kept eating the sugar cane.

The cane toad was brought in to eat insects. Instead, they ate just about everything else. They are still a problem today. ▶

 **Quick Check**

25. Why did farmers bring large toads to Australia over 70 years ago?

_____

_____

How does energy flow in a food web?

This diagram is a summary of what happens to the energy in a food web. The bottom of the diagram shows a producer—grass. Remember, producers get energy from the Sun. Producers make up the biggest part of the diagram.

The other levels are all consumers. Energy is passed to each level on top when the animal eats the food below it. The levels get smaller as you go to the top. Many producers are needed for the energy of just one living thing at the top.

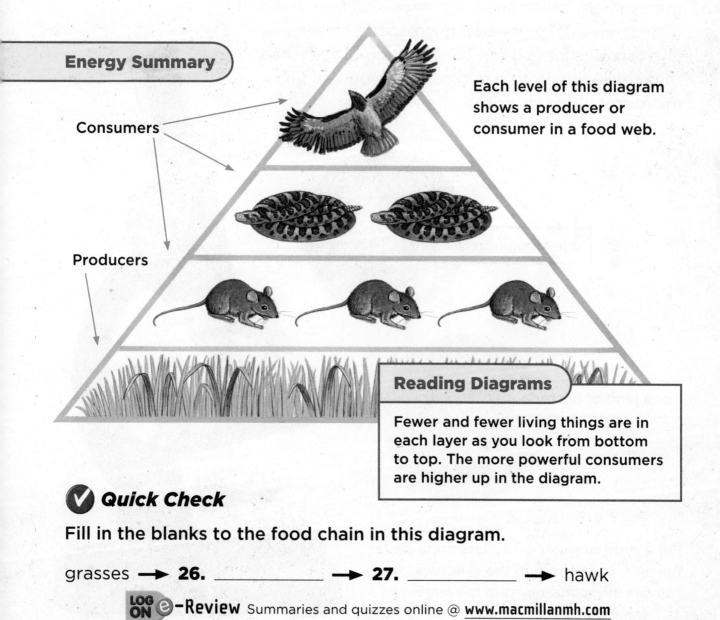

Energy Summary

Consumers

Producers

Each level of this diagram shows a producer or consumer in a food web.

Reading Diagrams

Fewer and fewer living things are in each layer as you look from bottom to top. The more powerful consumers are higher up in the diagram.

✔ Quick Check

Fill in the blanks to the food chain in this diagram.

grasses ➞ **26.** _____ ➞ **27.** _____ ➞ hawk

LOG ON **e-Review** Summaries and quizzes online @ **www.macmillanmh.com**

What is a microorganism?

You cannot see them, but there are tiny living things everywhere. They live on food. They live inside and on the outside of your body. They live in ponds, lakes, and oceans. They live in soil. They live on dust in the air.

Tiny living things too small to be seen with just our eyes are called **microorganisms** (migh•kroh•AWR•guh•niz•uhms). You need a microscope to see them. Microscopes let you see things much bigger than they really are. With a microscope, you can find microorganisms in a drop of pond water.

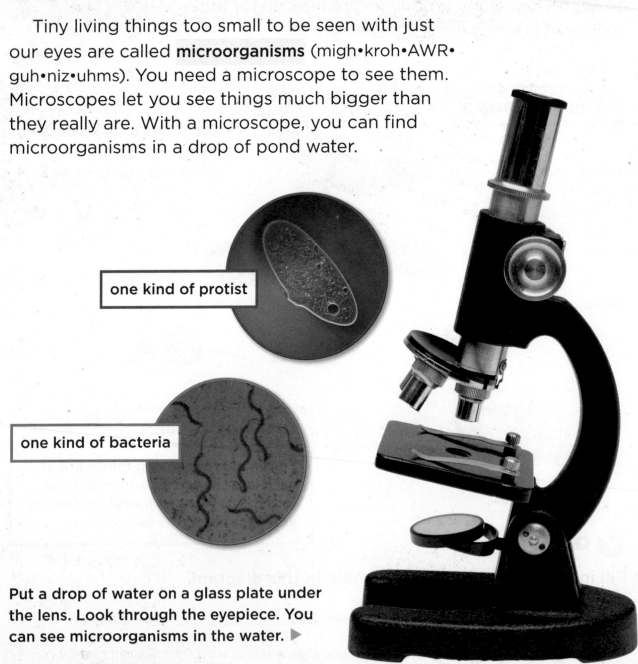

one kind of protist

one kind of bacteria

Put a drop of water on a glass plate under the lens. Look through the eyepiece. You can see microorganisms in the water. ▶

Among the smallest kinds of microorganisms are **bacteria** (bak•TEER•ee•uh). Some bacteria are helpful. For example, some help your body break down food that you eat. However, some bacteria cause disease.

Protists (PROH•tists) are microorganisms that are a little larger than bacteria. Some protists help you. They eat harmful bacteria. Other protists can cause disease.

Your body is protected against microorganisms that cause disease. You can help keep your body stay safe from them. For example, wash and cover a cut to keep harmful bacteria out of your body.

Stay Safe from Disease

disease	cause	how you can help
tooth decay	bacteria	brush and floss teeth
Lyme disease	bacteria in ticks	wear long pants on hikes

✓ Quick Check

28. How are bacteria and protists alike? _____

_____

_____

29. How are bacteria and protists different? _____

_____

_____

Which microorganisms are producers and consumers?

Some microorganisms act like plants. Some act like animals.

Producers

Plants are producers. Remember, producers are the first step in a food chain. They take in energy from the Sun and make their own food. They also give off oxygen to the air.

Some microorganisms are producers. For example, *algae* (AL•jee) are producers that grow in large numbers at the top of ponds, lakes, and the ocean. Algae are important because they make much of the oxygen for living things.

Algae and other tiny producers act like plants, but they are not plants. They do not have the parts plants have. They do not have roots, stems, and leaves.

▲ These algae are seen under a microscope. Unlike plants, they have no roots, stems, and leaves. However, they do make food and oxygen.

Consumers

Remember, animals cannot make their own food. Animals are consumers. They move about to get food.

Some microorganisms act like animals. For example, an *amoeba* (uh•MEE•buh) is a protist. It acts like an animal. It moves its body to get food. It can wrap around the food to catch it.

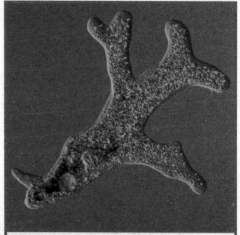

The body of an amoeba flows in different directions. The body seems to reach out toward food. The body can flow around the food.

Producers and Consumers

Euglena (yew•GLEE•nuh) is a protist that lives in ponds. It acts like a plant and like an animal. In sunlight, it can make its own food—like a plant. It can also move around to get food—like an animal.

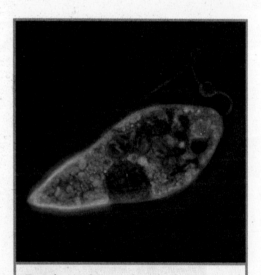

Euglena has a body part that looks like a tail. It whips this part as it moves.

☑ *Quick Check*

Complete this main idea chart.

Main Idea	Details
Tiny living things can act like plants or animals, or both.	Some can make food, like plants.
	30. _____

Which microorganisms are decomposers?

Remember, decomposers are the last step in a food chain. They break down dead plants and animals. The diagram shows three decomposers on a dead tree. One is a large living thing, the mushroom. The two other decomposers are microorganisms. They are mold and bacteria.

A mushroom is a fungus (FUNG•guhs). A **fungus** is a living thing that may look like a plant. However, a fungus does not make its own food as plants do. It gets food by feeding off a dead thing.

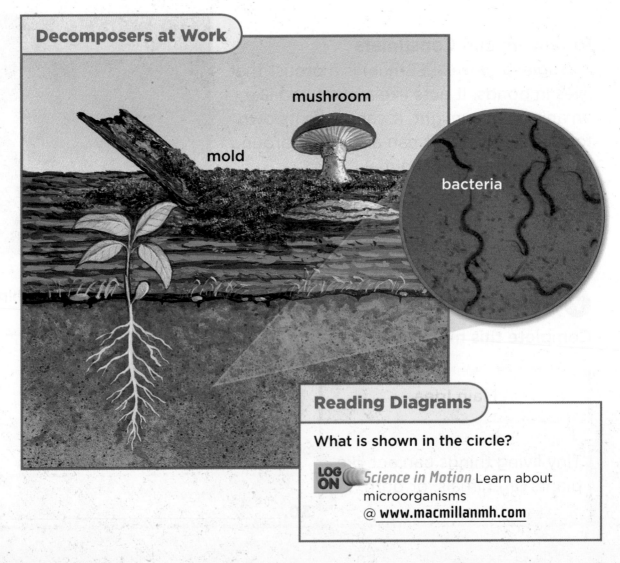

Decomposers at Work

mushroom

mold

bacteria

Reading Diagrams

What is shown in the circle?

LOG ON *Science in Motion* Learn about microorganisms @ **www.macmillanmh.com**

The diagram on page 24 shows two other decomposers: mold and bacteria. Both are microorganisms. Mold is a type of fungus. A single mold is too small to see. However, you can see mold growing in large numbers on dead wood and other once-living things. They make the once-living things rot.

Bacteria are much smaller than mold. You can see them only with a microscope. There may be billions of bacteria in just a teaspoonful of soil. Many bacteria in soil are decomposers.

When the tree is broken down, it becomes part of the soil. The soil is then ready for new plants to grow.

Molds are growing on this apple. Mold grow fast in warm temperatures.

 Quick Check

List the three decomposers in order from largest to smallest.

31. _____

32. _____

33. _____

LOG ON ℮-**Review** Summaries and quizzes online @ **www.macmillanmh.com**

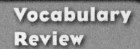

Living Things Need Energy

Choose the letter of the best answer.

1. One way to show how food chains in any place are linked together is to draw a(n)

   a. photosynthesis

   b. living thing

   c. food web

   d. producer

2. Microorganisms that are larger than bacteria are

   a. protists

   b. fungus

   c. producers

   d. consumers

3. An animal that eats both plants and animals is a(n)

   a. bacteria

   b. decomposer

   c. herbivore

   d. omnivore

4. Any living thing that makes, or produces, its own food is a(n)

   a. producer   c. bacteria

   b. protist   d. fungus

5. Everything that surrounds a living thing is called a(n)

   a. food chain

   b. competition

   c. food web

   d. environment

6. When animals try to get the same thing that others need or want, they

   a. produce   c. compete

   b. eat   d. surround

7. The way plants use sunlight to make food is called

   a. decomposer

   b. photosynthesis

   c. omnivore

   d. food chain

consumer	fungus	bacteria	herbivore
carnivore	decomposer	food chain	

Use each word just once to fill in the blanks.

1. A living thing that breaks down dead plants and animals

is called a(n) _____.

2. An animal that eats mostly plants is a(n)

_____.

3. The smallest of the microorganisms is

_____.

4. An animal that eats other animals is called a(n)

_____.

5. The path of energy in the form of food from one to

another is called the _____.

6. A plantlike living thing that breaks down dead plants

and animals is _____.

7. A living thing that eats other living things is a(n)

_____.

CHAPTER 2

Living Things and Their Environment

Vocabulary

 **ecosystem** all the living and nonliving things working together in an area

 **climate** the kind of weather an area has over time

 **emergent layer** the tops of trees in a rain forest

 **canopy** the layer just under the tops of the trees in a rain forest, where most plants and animals live

 **pollen** a powdery material that flowers need to make seeds

 **stamen** the part of a plant where pollen comes from

stamen

 **pistil** the part of a plant where seeds are made

pistil

 **pollination** the movement of pollen to the seed-making part of a flower

pollen

How do living things depend on one another and the environment?

 **nectar** a sweet liquid formed inside flowers

 **adaptation** a body feature or way of acting that helps a living thing survive in its environment

 **endangered** few left of this kind of living thing

 **camouflage** how a living thing might not be seen because it blends into its surroundings

 **extinct** none of this kind of living thing left alive today

 **mimicry** how an animal may look like some kind of other living thing

What is an ecosystem?

Plants grow from the soil. They need water to grow. Some birds use plants to make nests. Some animals eat plants. Tiny living things, bacteria, may break down dead plants. These are ways plants, animals, bacteria, soil, and water *interact*. *Interact* means "one thing uses or needs another."

All the parts interacting in any place make up an **ecosystem** (EK•oh•sis•tuhm). Some parts may be living. For example, plants are living. Some parts, such as water, are nonliving.

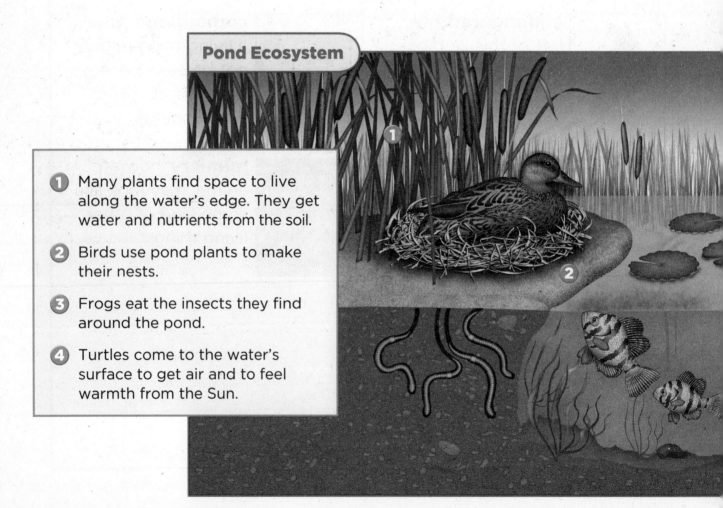

Pond Ecosystem

1. Many plants find space to live along the water's edge. They get water and nutrients from the soil.

2. Birds use pond plants to make their nests.

3. Frogs eat the insects they find around the pond.

4. Turtles come to the water's surface to get air and to feel warmth from the Sun.

Living Things	Nonliving Things
• animals—such as birds, frogs, turtles, fishes, crayfish, insects, earthworms • plants—such as lily pads on the water, cattails on the shore • tiny living things—such as algae and bacteria	• sunlight • air • water • soil • climate (KLIGH•mit) • **Climate** is the kind of weather an area has over time. The climate is the temperature and the amount of rain and snow the area has.

✔️ *Quick Check*

1. Cross out any part that is not a living part of a pond.

   duck   catfish   beetle   water   sunlight   frogs   air

2. List two more parts of a pond. _____

Reading Diagrams

Each number in the diagram has a matching statement at the left that tells how living and nonliving things interact.

What is a desert ecosystem?

All deserts are dry. They get little rain. Some deserts are hot. Others are cold. Some deserts are almost lifeless. Some have many living things. Living things of the deserts have ways of surviving the little water and the hot or cold temperatures.

California's Mojave Desert is dry and hot. It gets about 13 centimeters (5 inches) of rain a year. Many plants and animals can live here.

The fennec fox lives without water for a long time. It stays underground in the day and looks for food at night when it is cool.

The desert tortoise spends much of the time underground. That keeps it safe when temperatures change from day to night.

✔ Quick Check

3. How can deserts be different? _____

_____

What is a coral reef ecosystem?

Coral reefs are warm ecosystems. They are found in shallow water. Their temperatures stay warm all year, from 70 to 85°F (21 to 29°C). The warm temperatures allow many ocean animals to live here.

The reefs were made from the parts of tiny animals, coral polyps (POL•ips). After the animals die, their skeletons are left behind. The skeletons form the reefs.

Fishes swim across the reef. Many colorful sea animals grow attached to the reef. They may look like plants, but they are animals.

✔ Quick Check

Show how deserts and coral reefs are alike and different.

Coral Reefs (different)   **Alike**   **Deserts** (different)

are wet   4. Both are _____   5. _____

_____

_____

_____

What is a rain-forest ecosystem like?

Rain forests are hot and wet. They can get up to 457 centimeters (180 inches) of rain a year. Compare that to only 13 centimeters (5 inches) of rain a year in the Mojave Desert.

Although the soil is thin, these forests are thick with tall trees. Rain forests are filled with many kinds of life. Different living things make their homes at all parts of the trees, from the tops to the bottom.

squirrel monkeys

iguana

▲ The rain forest is made of different layers, from the sunny tops to the shady bottom.

Layers of the Rain Forest

layer	location	description
emergent layer (ee•MER•jent)	tops of tallest trees	• very sunny • high temperatures • strong winds
canopy (kan•UH•pee)	just below the tree tops	• sunny • most crowded with life, including snakes, tree frogs, and toucans
understory	beneath the canopy	• shady • home of jaguars, leopards, frogs and many insects
forest floor	bottom of the trees	• dark, little sunlight • filled with decomposers—living things that break down dead plants and animals

The forest floor is filled with dead leaves and other once-living things. Decomposers work quickly breaking them down and returning the remains to the soil.

✔️ *Quick Check*

Write the letter of the living things for each layer.

6. _____ canopy   **a.** decomposers

7. _____ understudy   **b.** snakes, toucans

8. _____ forest floor   **c.** leopards

How do animals depend on plants?

Plants can trap energy from the Sun. They use that energy to make their own food. As they make food, they also give off oxygen.

Plants as Food

Animals cannot make their own food. One way or another, animals depend on plants for food. They also depend on plants for oxygen.

Some animals eat plants directly. For example, rabbits eat leaves. Some beetles eat roots and stems. Monkeys and birds eat fruits and seeds. Snails and earthworms feed off dead plants.

Some animals are meat eaters. However, even meat eaters depend on plants because they may eat animals that are plant eaters.

▲ Squirrels use nuts for food. The nuts are seeds, parts of plants.

◀ Caterpillars eat leaves as a source of food energy.

Plants as Shelter

Many animals depend on plants for shelter. Many squirrels, for example, may live in tree holes. They line the holes with leaves. Many birds build nests in trees. They use twigs and leaves for the nests. They use the nests to keep their young safe.

Many animals hide in plants to stay safe. For example, a rabbit jumps into bushes if danger is near. Leafhoppers hide in grass.

Grass as Protection

Reading Photos

The color and shape of the snake blends the animal in with the grass.

✔ Quick Check

Fill in one idea in each empty box to explain the summary.

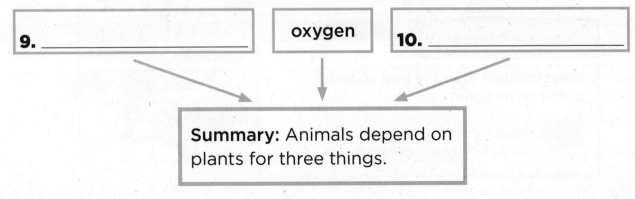

9. _____

oxygen

10. _____

Summary: Animals depend on plants for three things.

How do some plants depend on animals?

Flowering plants make seeds when they reproduce. Animals can help the plants make seeds.

A flowering plant needs **pollen** (POL•uhn) to make seeds. Pollen is like a fine powder. The diagram shows what happens to pollen.

- Find the **stamen** (STAY•muhn) in the diagram. The stamen is the part of a flower that makes pollen. Pollen collects at the tip.
- Find the **pistil**. The pistil is where seeds are made.
- A flower can make a seed only if pollen reaches the pistil. The diagram shows one way pollen reaches a pistil.

Pollination

pistil

stamen

pollen

Reading Diagrams

What happens after the bird collects pollen on its body?

LOG ON *Science in Motion* Watch how pollination occurs @ **www.macmillanmh.com**

Pollination (POHL•uh•nay•shuhn) is the movement of pollen to the pistil. Wind can blow pollen from a stamen to a pistil.

Also, animals can move pollen:

- Birds, bats, and many insects travel from flower to flower. They collect a sweet drink from flowers called **nectar** (NEK•tar).
- When an animal visits a flower to collect nectar, pollen can rub onto its body.
- When the animal visits another flower, the pollen drops off.

Animals carry seeds to places where seeds can grow. Some animals carry seeds on their fur. In time the seeds fall onto the ground.

Plants store seeds inside fruits. Animals may eat a fruit that has seeds inside. The seeds are left on the ground when animals leave waste.

Pollen from the flower collects on the bee's body as the bee looks for nectar.

This iguana eats a fruit with seeds in it.

✔ Quick Check

Fill in the blanks to tell two ways how plants depend on animals.

Animals can move **11.** _____ and carry

12. _____.

How can ecosystems change?

Remember, an ecosystem is made up both of living and nonliving things working together. Living things, like plants, need nonliving things, like soil, water, and sunlight. When one part of an ecosystem changes, such as the amount of water, all parts of the ecosystem can change.

Ecosystems can change over time. They can become hotter or drier. They can become colder or warmer. A lake can dry up or fill in. Any kind of change can make it harder for living things to survive.

▲ Lake Tahoe in California has changed slowly over thousands of years to look the way it does today. It also changes from season to season.

▲ Cars give off wastes that causes pollution.

Natural Events

Changes in weather can affect ecosystems. Storms, like hurricanes, can destroy ecosystems. Lightning can start a fire and turn a forest to ash.

The climate may change. Climate is the weather over time. An area may become drier, for example. A grassland can dry up.

Humans

People can cut down forests to make farms or build towns. Entire ecosystems can be destroyed. People can cause pollution (pol•LEW•shuhn). Pollution means putting materials to the air, land, or water that can make it harder for plants and animals to live.

✔ Quick Check

Two ways ecosystems can change are:

13. _____ and

14. _____.

What happens when ecosystems change?

A fire destroys a forest. What happens to the living things that are left?

• Some living things change they way they live. They may find new kinds of food. They may find news ways to build homes.
• Some animals move to other places.
• Some kinds of animals may slowly die out.

A living thing that has few of its kind left is **endangered** (en•DAYN•juhrd). A living thing is **extinct** (ek•STINGT) when it dies out and there are none of its kind left.

 **Quick Check**

Fill in the "effect" side to tell two ways the deer can keep alive after a fire destroys their home.

Cause →	Effect
Fire →	**15.** _____
Fire →	**16.** _____

How can people protect ecosystems?

People are finding ways to protect ecosystems. For example they are finding ways to cut down on pollution. People are looking for new fuels and passing laws against polluting the land, water and air.

Laws are also being passed to protect forests from being cut down. Laws can protect animals from being hunted.

People had destroyed the homes of the California condor. Now people are carefully raising them in safe environments.

✅ Quick Check

Fill in the right side of the table.

Saving Ecosystems	
What Can I Do?	**How It Helps**
Turn off water while brushing teeth.	to save water
Do not litter.	**17.** _____
Walk or ride a bike instead of riding a car.	**18.** _____

LOG ON ℮-Review Summaries and quizzes online @ www.macmillanmh.com

What is an adaptation?

A giraffe's long neck helps it reach high branches. A dolphin's tail and fins help it swim quickly in the ocean. An eagle's keen eyesight helps it spot food. These body features are adaptations (a•dap•TAY•shuhnz). **Adaptations** are body features or ways of acting that help living things survive in their environment.

Adaptations can help animals move and catch food. Adaptations can help animals and plants live in hot or cold climates.

▲ A dragonfly's wings help these insects fly fast so they can catch food and escape danger.

A giraffe's long neck helps the animal reach leaves to eat. It also gives the animal a view of danger that may be coming, such as a lion.

Some adaptations help living things stay safe. **Camouflage** (KAM•uh•flahzh) is an adaptation that helps a living thing blend into its environment. For example, if a deer stays still against a brown background, it may not be seen.

Some animals hide by looking like other living things. This adaptation is **mimicry** (MIM•i•kree).

The Indian leaf butterfly is an example of mimicry. Its color may help you spot the insect. However, its shape makes it look like a leaf.

✓ Quick Check

Two adaptations that help this eagle catch a fish are

19. _____

20. _____

barrel cactus

Storing water The barrel cactus has a thick, waxy skin and thick, round stem. These adaptations help it store water in its stem. The prickly spines keep animals from biting into the plant to get the water.

wildflowers

Seeds Desert plants bloom quickly after a sudden rain. The bright colors attract insects. The insects help in pollination.

What are some adaptations in a desert?

Deserts get less than 25 centimeters (10 inches) of rain a year. Some places get more than that in a month. Adaptations help desert plants survive dry conditions.

More Desert Plants

Creosote (KREE•oh•soht) bushes have shallow roots. These roots help the plant take in water from the little rain that falls.

Ocotillo (oh•koh•TEE•oh) plants drop their leaves during very dry times to keep from drying out. Leaves grow back after the next rainfall.

kangaroo rat

chameleon

Storing water Many animals have kidneys. Kidneys help the body get rid of liquid wastes. However, the kangaroo rat's kidneys also help store water in the animal's body

Temperature control A chameleon (kah•MEE•lee•uhn) raises its belly off the hot desert ground as a way of cooling down.

Desert animals have adaptations that help them survive with little water. In hot deserts, animals have adaptations to help them stay cool.

More Desert Animals

Many desert animals, including the great horned owl are active at night when it is cooler. They rest or sleep during the day.

The jackrabbit has very long, thin ears to help keep cool. The blood carries body heat into the ears. The blood loses heat as it flows through the ears.

✔ Quick Check

Two living things that have adaptations for storing water are:

21. _____   **22.** _____

Two animals that have adaptations for surviving in heat are:

23. _____   **24.** _____

What are adaptations in the arctic and in oceans?

In the arctic and the oceans, living things have ways of surviving the most harsh conditions.

The Arctic

polar bear

Skin and fur The outer fur of a polar bear is waterproof. The thick inner fur keeps the bear warm. Black skin beneath the white fur helps the bear take in heat from the Sun.

arctic fox

Camouflage The arctic fox in winter has a white coat. The coat helps it blend in with the snow. In summer its coat is brown.

Other Arctic Animals and Plants

The large size of a musk ox and polar bear helps them to keep warm.

Arctic plants grow low near the ground. This adaptation protects them from the wind. They often have bright flowers. The colors attract animals that help in pollination.

The Oceans

whale

Blubber A whale has blubber, a thick layer of fat. Blubber helps keep a whale's body warm in cold ocean water.

leafy seadragon

Mimicry The leafy seadragon is a kind of fish. However, it looks like the seaweed that surrounds it.

✓ Quick Check

Arctic (different)   Alike   Ocean (different)

25. _____   26. _____   28. _____

_____

27. _____

_____

LOG ON **e-Review** Summaries and quizzes online @ www.macmillanmh.com

Living Things and Their Environment

Fill the missing words in the blanks below. Then find
and circle those words in the puzzle at the bottom.

1. The layer just under the tops of the trees in a rain forest, where most

plants and animals live _____

2. The part of a plant where seeds are made _____

3. A sweet liquid formed inside flowers _____

4. The kind of weather an area has over time _____

5. A living thing that has died out and there are none of its kind left

today _____

6. A living thing that has few of its kind left _____

7. The part of a plant that makes pollen _____

```
T  R  C  S  C  N  Z  D  T  M  T  U  E  M  Y
M  N  E  F  E  C  G  K  J  N  M  N  X  V  P
C  A  E  C  Y  O  R  X  F  D  B  Q  T  O  O
S  L  T  M  R  Z  F  Z  O  P  T  K  I  F  N
U  A  I  W  A  I  Z  L  H  U  L  N  N  Z  A
R  H  L  M  G  T  Q  C  D  E  H  I  C  E  C
Y  I  B  M  A  V  S  U  S  W  A  P  T  Q  H
K  M  B  E  T  T  U  F  U  W  S  S  I  C  W
E  N  D  A  N  G  E  R  E  D  I  V  B  T  N
P  T  Z  B  Q  V  G  B  L  I  T  S  I  P  S
```

| a. camouflage | c. mimicry | e. pollination | g. ecosystem |
| b. emergent layer | d. adaptation | f. pollen | |

Match the correct letter with the description.

1. _____ The movement of pollen to the seed-making part of a flower

2. _____ The tops of trees in a rain forest

3. _____ How a living thing might not have been seen because it blends into its surroundings

4. _____ A powdery material that flowers need to make seeds

5. _____ All the living and nonliving things working together in an area

6. _____ How an animal might look like some kind of other living thing

7. _____ A body feature or way of acting that helps a living thing survive in its environment

Answer the question. Use at least one word from the box in your answer.

8. What are some ways that animals protect themselves?

_____

_____

CHAPTER 3

Rocks and Minerals

Vocabulary

 **mineral** one of the parts that a rock is made of

 ore a rock that contains a useful mineral

 **luster** the way something shines in the light

 **magma** hot, melted rock beneath Earth's surface

 **streak** the color of the powder made when a mineral is scratched on white tile

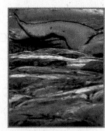 **lava** magma that reaches Earth's surface

 **hardness** the ability of a mineral to scratch another mineral

 igneous rock a rock formed from hot, melted rock that cools and hardens

The Big Idea

What are rocks and minerals and where do they come from?

 sediment tiny broken bits of rocks, plants, bones, and shells

 **sedimentary rock** a rock formed from tiny pieces of broken rocks pressed together

 **fossil** the remains of a once living thing from long ago

 **metamorphic rock** a rock formed from another rock that is being squeezed and heated

 **rock cycle** the continual changing of one kind of rock into another kind

What is a mineral?

Pick up a rock—for example, a chunk of granite. You can see that it is made of small pieces of different colors and shapes.

The pieces in granite are minerals (MIN•uhr•uhlz). **Minerals** are the parts that rocks are made of. Minerals are the building blocks of rocks. Rocks may be made of many minerals or just one.

There are thousands of minerals. They have different shapes and colors. Here are the four minerals that make up granite.

Minerals in Granite

▲ Mineral: Quartz many colors or colorless

▲ Mineral: Feldspar green to pink to blue

Rock: Granite is a rock made of several minerals.

▲ Mineral: Hornblende dark, black to green

▲ Mineral: Mica brown, clear, or black It peels into flakes

✔ *Quick Check*

1. How are minerals different?	**2.** How are minerals alike?
_____	_____
_____	_____
_____	_____

What are minerals used for?

People can take minerals out of rocks. Then we can use the minerals in many ways. From toothpaste to eyeglasses, minerals are used to make many things we use every day.

Many minerals that we use are from ores (AWRZ). **Ores** are rocks that contain useful minerals. The mineral aluminum for example comes from the ore bauxite (BAWK•sight). We use aluminum for cans, pots and pans, and even baseball bats.

Diamonds and rubies are gems, minerals valued for beauty, used for jewelry.

Ways We Use Minerals

mineral	uses
quartz	glass and glass products
gypsum	drywall (for making walls in building)
copper	electrical wires; pots and pans

✔️ Quick Check

3. Why are minerals important? _____

_____

How are minerals identified?

When you *identify* something, you are able to name it. How can you identify a mineral?

The color on the outside of a mineral is not the best clue to identify a mineral. Two different minerals can have the same color. For example, calcite and quartz can both be white. Any one mineral may come in many colors. Quartz can be white, purple, or pink.

Luster

Luster can help you identify minerals. **Luster** is the way something shines in the light. Some minerals have a shiny or metallic luster, like a metal spoon. Other minerals have a nonmetallic luster. They may be dull or glassy.

Splitting

Some minerals split, or break along flat surfaces. Calcite, for example, splits into boxlike shapes. Remember from page 54 that mica splits into flakes. Some minerals do not split evenly.

Pyrite (PIGH•right) was called "fool's gold." It has a yellow color and a metallic luster like gold.

Calcite splits into boxlike shapes.

Some minerals, such as quartz, do not split along flat surfaces.

Streak

A helpful clue to identify a mineral is its streak. **Streak** is the color of the powder left when a mineral is rubbed along a rough white tile. Some minerals leave a streak that is the same color of the mineral. Others leave a streak that does not look like the color of the mineral. Pyrite has a yellow color but leaves a greenish-black streak.

Hematite has a black surface. However, it leaves a red streak.

Comparing Color and Streak

Mineral	Color of Outside of Mineral	Streak
gold	yellow	yellow
pyrite	yellow	greenish-black
calcite	white or colorless	always white

✓ Quick Check

Match the clues with the letter of the mineral.

4. _____ black color, reddish streak

5. _____ metallic luster, greenish-black streak

6. _____ splits into flakes

7. _____ splits in boxlike shapes

a. mica

b. calcite

c. hematite

d. pyrite

What is hardness?

The hardness of a mineral can also help you identify it. **Hardness** is the ability of one mineral to scratch another mineral.

Each mineral has a hardness number. Look at the the chart. Talc is number 1, the softest. Diamond is number 10, the hardest.

A mineral can scratch any other mineral that has the same or a lower hardness number. For example, calcite, number 3, can scratch, any mineral with a hardness number that is 3 or less. Calcite can scratch gypsum and talc.

You can use everyday items to find the hardness of minerals. Your fingernail can scratch gypsum and talc. A penny can scratch calcite, gypsum, and talc.

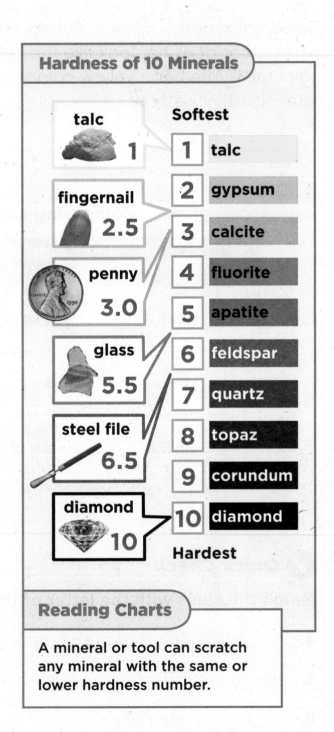

Hardness of 10 Minerals

	Softest	
talc 1	1	talc
fingernail 2.5	2	gypsum
	3	calcite
penny 3.0	4	fluorite
	5	apatite
glass 5.5	6	feldspar
	7	quartz
steel file 6.5	8	topaz
	9	corundum
diamond 10	10	diamond
	Hardest	

Reading Charts

A mineral or tool can scratch any mineral with the same or lower hardness number.

Mineral Identification Table

Mineral	Hardness	Luster	Streak	Color	Splits
quartz	7	nonmetallic	none	colorless, white, pink, purple, brown	breaks unevenly
mica	2–2.5	nonmetallic	none	dark brown, black, or silver-white	flakes
calcite	3	nonmetallic	white	colorless, white	boxlike shapes

The table sums up the clues you can use to identify some minerals. For example, quartz and calcite may both be white. However, quartz is much harder than calcite.

✓ Quick Check

Tell how mica and calcite are alike and different.

8. Mica can have a _____ color

and splits into _____.

9. They both have a hardness of _____

or less and have a nonmetallic _____.

10. Calcite can have a _____

color and splits into _____.

LOG ON e-Review Summaries and quizzes online @ www.macmillanmh.com

How are igneous rocks formed?

The rocks you know are solids. However, deep below Earth's surface, rock is very hot. It is melted into a liquid. Hot, melted rock below Earth's surface is **magma** (MAG•muh). In some places, magma reaches the surface, as you see in the diagram. Magma that reaches the surface is **lava** (LA•vuh).

Above or even below the surface, the melted rock can cool off. When it cools off, it hardens into a solid, igneous (IG•nee•us) rock. **Igneous rock** is rock formed when hot, melted rock cools and hardens.

How Igneous Rocks Form

Some igneous rocks such as granite are formed when magma cools below Earth's surface.

Some igneous rocks such as rhyolite are formed when lava cools above Earth's surface.

lava

magma

Underground Rocks

Magma can rise up from deep underground. It can cool off underground before it gets to the surface. The magma may take many years to cool off underground. It forms igneous rocks that have large pieces of minerals inside. Example:

- granite

Rocks Above Ground

Above Earth's surface, lava cools off quickly, in hours or even minutes. The minerals inside the rock are small. They may be so small that you cannot see each of them. Example:

- rhyolite (RIGH•uh•light)

✔ Quick Check

Write the name of a rock next to each description. Use each rock twice.

rhyolite   granite

11. forms underground _____

12. forms above ground _____

13. has small minerals inside _____

14. has large minerals inside _____

Reading Diagrams

How can you tell from the diagram that magma must be hot?

LOG ON *Science in Motion* Watch how igneous rocks form @ **www.macmillanmh.com**

What are some properties of igneous rocks?

There are many different igneous rocks. They may have different minerals inside. The minerals are large pieces if the rock was formed underground. The minerals are small if the rock was formed above ground.

Granite

- formed underground
- is made of several different minerals
- has large minerals that make it feel rough (coarse)
- comes in many colors because of different colors of minerals inside

Granite

Pumice (PUM·is)

- formed above ground
- has tiny holes inside from trapped gases
- very lightweight
- feels scratchy, crumbly

Pumice

Obsidian (uhb·SID·ee·uhn)

- formed above ground
- feels very smooth like glass
- has a glassy shine (luster)
- dark in color, often black

Obsidian

The Great Wall of China was made from blocks of granite. It was built over 2,000 years ago.

Uses of Igneous Rocks

Igneous rocks are useful in many ways because of their properties.

- Granite is hard and long lasting. It is used to make roads, sidewalks, buildings, and bridges.
- Pumice is scratchy and rough. It is used in cleansers to scrub off dirt.

✔ Quick Check

Write the name of each rock once next to each description.

pumice   obsidian   granite

15. hard, used to make buildings _____

16. scratchy, used in cleansers _____

17. like shiny, smooth glass _____

LOG ON e-Review Summaries and quizzes online @ **www.macmillanmh.com**

How are sedimentary rocks formed?

Some rocks are formed from sediments (SED•uh•mentz). **Sediments** are tiny broken bits of rocks, plants, bones, shells, and other animal materials. Rocks formed when sediments are pressed togther into layers are **sedimentary rocks**.

You can see the layers of sedimentary rocks along the Grand Canyon. The colors of these layers come from different kinds of sediments.

How Layers Form

Layers of sedimentary rocks form in three steps.

- Moving things (wind, rivers, and streams) pick up and carry sediment.
- The moving things drop off sediment and layers form.
- Layers build up, one on top of another. Layers above press down on the layers below. The sediment in the lower layers are cemented together. They become sedimentary rock.

In the sediment that forms in a sedimentary rock, there are often pieces of living things, such as leaves and bones. The remains of living things from long ago are **fossils**.

Layers of Sediments

Ⓐ
Ⓑ
Ⓒ
Ⓓ

Reading Diagrams

Younger layers are found above older layers.

This fossil was found in sedimentary rock that was once underwater.

 Quick Check

Complete the diagram. With just a few words in each step, summarize how layers form.

First **18.** _____

↓

Next Drop off; layers form.

↓

Last **19.** _____

What are some properties of sedimentary rocks?

There are many different sedimentary rocks. They are made from different kinds and sizes of sediments. Some are softer than others. Some have layers. Some do not show layers. Many kinds contain fossils.

Limestone

- formed at bottoms of oceans
- formed from remains of once-living things, such as bones and shells
- usually white, chalky
- often has fossils

Limestone often contains fossils, such as this ancient fish.

Sandstone

- formed from bits of sand cemented together
- sand is made up of the mineral quartz
- may show ripples if it was formed underwater

This sample of sandstone is reddish from rust. The rust is cementing the sand together. You can see thin layers inside the rock.

Conglomerate (kuhn·GLOM·uhr·it)

- formed from rounded pebbles and stones, which may once have been carried by streams or rivers
- has several sizes and kinds of sediment
- looks chunky and feels rough

Conglomerate shows chunks of other rocks. No layers are visible.

Uses of Sedimentary Rocks

Sedimentary rocks have useful properties.

- Limestone is soft. It is used to make chalk.
- Shale can be molded. It is used for bricks and pottery.
- Soft coal was formed from the remains of ancient plants. The energy stored in soft coal is from ancient plants.

Sedimentary rocks help us piece together Earth's past. Fossils in these rocks show what life was like in the past.

Soft coal contains stored energy from plants that lived long ago.

✓ Quick Check

20. How could you identify a piece of sandstone?

_____

21. How could you identify a piece of conglomerate?

_____

LOG ON e-Review Summaries and quizzes online @ www.macmillanmh.com

How are metamorphic rocks formed?

Below Earth's surface are many layers of rocks. Layers near the top press down on deeper layers. This pressing squeezes deeper layers together. Also, the deeper layers are heated by the hot magma that is nearby.

Deep inside Earth, rocks that are squeezed and heated can change into other rocks called **metamorphic** (met•uh•MAWR•fik) **rocks**. Metamorphic rocks can be formed from any kind of rocks.

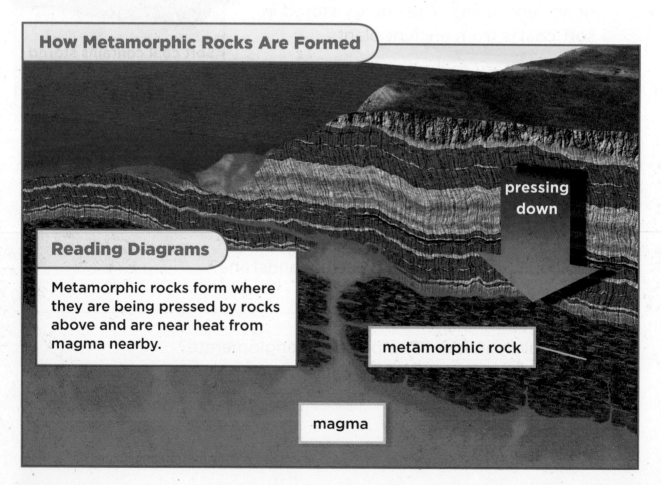

How Metamorphic Rocks Are Formed

pressing down

Reading Diagrams

Metamorphic rocks form where they are being pressed by rocks above and are near heat from magma nearby.

metamorphic rock

magma

Rocks Make-Overs

One metamorphic rock you may know is slate. Slate is a hard rock used to make chalkboards and roofs. It is formed from a soft sedimentary rock, shale. When shale is squeezed and heated deep inside Earth it becomes slate. Slate, in turn, can change into *another* metamorphic rock, schist (SHIST).

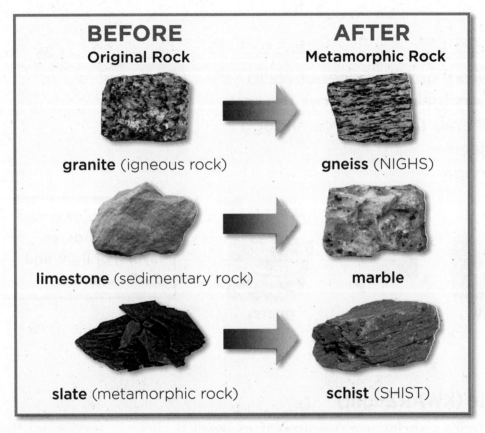

BEFORE
Original Rock

AFTER
Metamorphic Rock

granite (igneous rock) → **gneiss** (NIGHS)

limestone (sedimentary rock) → **marble**

slate (metamorphic rock) → **schist** (SHIST)

✔ *Quick Check*

Fill in the boxes to show how metamorphic rocks are formed

Deeper rocks are squeezed by rocks above.

Deeper rocks are **22.** _____

Summary

Any rock can be changed into **23.** _____

What are the properties of some metamorphic rocks?

Metamorphic rocks have many different properties because they come from many other kinds of rocks. They may be squeezed and heated differently and end up with different properties.

Gneiss

- forms from granite (igneous rock)
- has layers (or bands) across the rock
- has minerals that are large enough to be seen
- feels rough

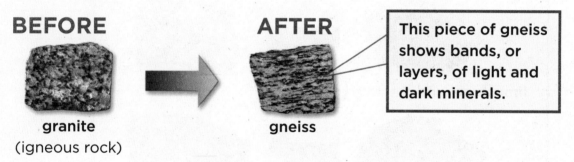

BEFORE

granite
(igneous rock)

AFTER

gneiss

This piece of gneiss shows bands, or layers, of light and dark minerals.

Quartzite (KWARZ·ight)

- forms from sandstone (sedimentary rock)
- does not have layers (or bands)
- has small minerals inside
- feels smoother than gneiss

BEFORE

sandstone
(sedimentary rock)

AFTER

quartzite

Quartzite comes in many colors but most often looks glassy.

Marble

- forms from limestone (sedimentary rock)
- does not have layers (or bands)
- can have small minerals and feel smooth
- can have larger minerals and feel rough

BEFORE **AFTER**

Marble comes in many colors, but is often white.

limestone
(sedimentary rock)

marble

Slate

- forms from shale (sedimentary rock)
- has layers
- has small minerals and feels smooth

BEFORE **AFTER**

Slate has thin, flat layers

shale
(sedimentary rock)

slate

Quick Check

Circle the letter of the correct answer.

18. Quarzite

    a. feels very rough **b.** has layers **c.** feels smoother than gneiss

19. Marble

    a. always is green **b.** may feel rough **c.** has layers

20. Gneiss

    a. has layers **b.** feels smooth **c.** has small minerals

What are some uses of metamorphic rock?

Metamorphic rocks are useful because of their properties. They are used for buildings, sidewalks, statues, and jewelry. Here are some examples:

- Marble is used for buildings and statues because it does not split when it is carved.
- Slate is used for roofs because it is waterproof. It is used for walkways because it is hard and smooth.
- Quartzite is used for making glass and pottery. It is also used for tile floors and stone walls.

A hard form of coal is a metamorphic rock. It is formed from soft coal, which is a sedimentary rock. Hard coal comes from deeper inside Earth than soft coal. It burns cleaner and longer than soft coal.

▲ **This roof is built with shingles. The shingles are small flat pieces of slate.**

 Quick Check

Match the rock and its use.

21. _____ slate

a. burned for energy

22. _____ marble

b. used to make statutes

23. _____ quartzite

c. used to make glass

24. _____ hard coal

d. used to make roofs

How can you be a rock detective?

How can you tell if a rock is an igneous rock? How can you tell a sedimentary rock from a metamorphic rock? You can identify each kind of rock by several clues.

Sedimentary Rocks

- may contain fossils
- often have layers and can break apart

Fossils are found in sedimentary rocks, such as shale, sandstone, or limestone.

Igneous Rocks

- are usually hard
- do not have layers
- may have minerals that twinkle in the light
- may look glassy (obsidian)

Metamorphic Rocks

- may have colored bands

✔ Quick Check

Match the rock and its clue.

25. _____ metamorphic

26. _____ igneous

27. _____ sedimentary

a. may have fossils

b. colored bands

c. is hard and has no layers

The Rock Cycle

Rocks are changing all the time. Any rock is changing into another kind of rock. The continual changing of one kind of rock into another kind is the **rock cycle**. The arrows shows some of the ways kinds of rocks are changing into each other all the time.

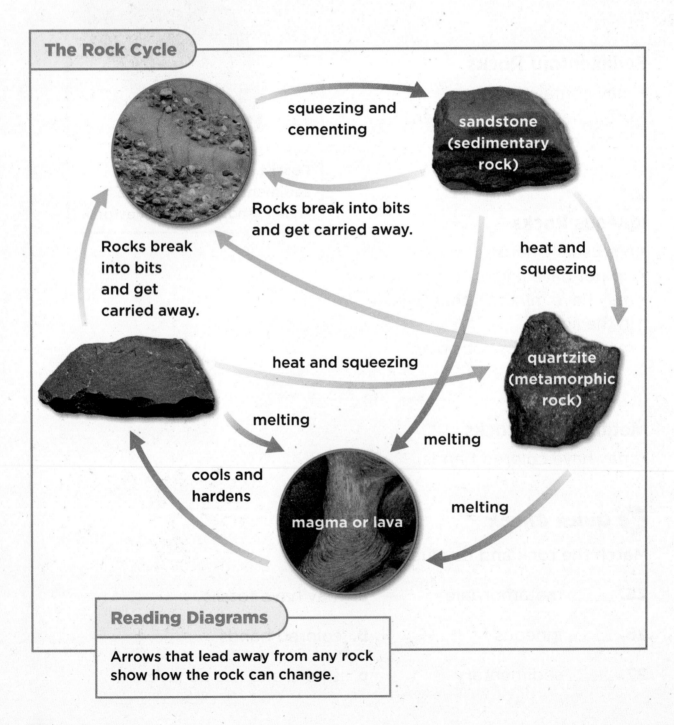

The Rock Cycle

squeezing and cementing

sandstone (sedimentary rock)

Rocks break into bits and get carried away.

Rocks break into bits and get carried away.

heat and squeezing

heat and squeezing

quartzite (metamorphic rock)

melting

melting

cools and hardens

magma or lava

melting

Reading Diagrams

Arrows that lead away from any rock show how the rock can change.

How to Read the Rock Cycle

Put your finger on any picture of a rock in the rock cycle. Find the arrows that lead away from the picture. Here is one pathway, following just the outer arrows:

1. Start with "magma or lava" at the bottom of the rock cycle.

2. Follow the blue arrow to the left. Magma or lava cools and hardens and becomes igneous rock.

3. Follow the green arrow leading up from igneous rock to the rock bits. Igneous rocks break into bits and get carried away.

4. Follow the purple arrow leading away from the rock bits. The bits can be pressed and cemented into a sedimentary rock.

5. Follow the gold arrow leading down from sedimentary rock. A sedimentary rock can be heated and squeezed to form a metamorphic rock.

Now follow some of the arrows *inside* the diagram.

✔ Quick Check

Sandstone (sedimentary rock) has three arrows pointing away from it. Read the arrows to tell three things that can happen to sedimentary rock.

28. _____

29. _____

30. _____

Rocks and Minerals

Complete the sentences below. Fill in each blank with one letter.

1. The ability of a mineral to scratch another mineral is called

__ O __ O __ __ __ __ .

2. A rock that is formed from another rock that is squeezed and

heated is __ __ __ O __ __ __ __ __ __ __ __   __ __ __ __ .

3. Chalk is a __ __ O O __ __ __ O __ __ __   __ __ __ __ that is
formed from tiny pieces of fossil shells.

4. Some igneous rocks are formed from O __ __ __ __ beneath Earth's
crust that has cooled and hardened.

5. Useful minerals can be mined from O __ __ .

6. A rock is made of one or more __ O O __ __ __ __ __ .

Write out all the letters that are in the circles.

__ __ __ __ __ __ __ __ __ __ __

**Use the letters from inside the circles above to name two minerals
described below. Clue: Look at the table in page 58.**

7. If you add the hardness of these two minerals, the sum is 11.

_____

_____

Use the clues below to fill in the crossword puzzle.

ACROSS

2. a rock formed from hot, melted rock that cools and hardens

3. the continual changing of one kind of rock into another kind

5. magma that reaches Earth's surface

6. the remains of a once living thing from long ago

7. tiny broken bits of rocks, plants, bones, and shells

DOWN

1. a part that a rock is made of

4. the way something shines in the light

7. the color of the powder made when a mineral is scratched on white tile

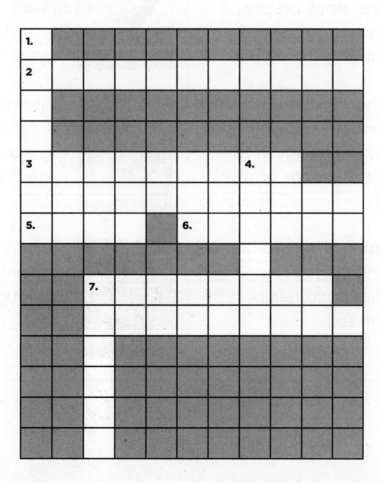

CHAPTER 4

Slow Changes on Earth

Vocabulary

 **weathering** breaking down rocks into small pieces

 **horizon** a layer of soil

 **physical weathering** breaking down rocks into small pieces by hitting them or making them split

 **erosion** carrying away broken pieces of rock

 **chemical weathering** breaking down rocks by chemicals in the air, water, or ground.

 **deposition** dropping off pieces of rock that were carried by wind, water, or ice

 **humus** rotted plant and animal remains that becomes part of the soil

 **plain** a flat stretch of land without any hills or mountains

What causes Earth's surface to change slowly?

landform any natural feature on Earth's surface

canyon a deep, narrow landform with steep sides, usually with a river running through it

valley the low land between hills or mountains

delta land built from rock pieces dropped off at the end of a river

barrier island long, narrow land built up from sand dropped off shore

sand dune a hill built from sand that is carried and dropped off by wind

glacier a large moving sheet of ice

What is weathering?

Rocks everywhere are slowly breaking down into small pieces. For example, wind, freezing, and even the growth of plants can cause a rock to break. The breaking down of rocks into small pieces is **weathering** (WETH•uhr•ing).

Weathering can happen in many ways. **Physical weathering** is breaking down rock by hitting them or an any other way making them split apart. Wind and rain are two main causes of physical weathering.

▲ Physical weathering slowly drilled these holes in solid rocks in Arches National Park.

Here are some causes of physical weathering:

- **Freezing and Melting** Water from rain or snow can seep into cracks in rocks. If the water freezes, ice forms. The ice can widen the cracks. Later the ice melts back into liquid water. Freezing and melting over and over break the rock apart.

- **Plants** Plant roots can grow into cracks in rocks and cause them to widen. Eventually the rock splits apart.

- **Peeling Off.** The surface of some huge rocks may peel off into large flakes.

- **Wind** Wind can carry sand and small rocks. Wind-driven sand and rocks act like slow drills. They drill into softer rocks.

Roots growing into a crack in a rock can slowly split the rock apart.

The surface of this mountain, Half Dome, peeled away.

✔ Quick Check

Describe how each of the following causes weathering.

1. Freezing _____

_____

2. Plant roots _____

_____

3. Wind driven sand _____

_____

What are some other causes of weathering?

You may have seen rust on a bicycle fender. Rust forms slowly and makes the fender crumble. Rust can also form in rocks.

Rust in rocks is a kind of chemical weathering. **Chemical weathering** happens when chemicals in the air, water, or land break down rocks. Here are some examples.

Oxygen

Here's how rusting can happen in rocks:

- Oxygen from the air mixes with water.
- The oxygen and water seep into a rock.
- If a rock has the mineral iron in it, oxygen forms rust in the rock. A rusted rock crumbles.

Anything that contains the mineral iron can rust when oxygen touches the iron. The rusted object crumbles away.

Acids

Acids are chemicals that can gradually eat away rocks. Acids seep into soil from rotting plants. Water seeping though the soil can pick up the acids. When acids come into contact with some kinds of rocks, it can gradually eat away the rocks.

Carbon Dioxide

Carbon dioxide is a gas in the air. It mixes with rainwater and forms an acid. This acid can seep through limestone and eat away a hole in the rock. Over many years, the hole slowly gets bigger and becomes a cave.

Carbon dioxide also comes from rotting remains of animals and plants. Rainwater soaks through the remains, picks up the gas, and forms the acid. The acid then can seep though the soil and eat away holes in rocks.

Weathered Limestone

The drip-like formations from the roof of a limestone cave come from water and acid dripping into the cave.

 Quick Check

Fill in the **diagram** to show how chemical weathering and physical weathering are alike and different.

Physical Weathering
(different)

Alike

Chemical Weathering
(different)

caused by freezing, plants, peeling, and wind

4. _____

5. caused by _____

How is soil formed?

What happens to rocks that get broken down into smaller and smaller pieces. In time, the pieces become part of soil.

Soil consists of:

- broken down pieces of rock
- **humus** (HYEW•muhs), which is rotted plants and animals material
- water
- air
- bacteria, some of the tiniest living things (which can be seen only with a microscope)
- plants and animals living in the top layer.

Over time, soil forms layers called **horizons**. Horizons are different from each other.

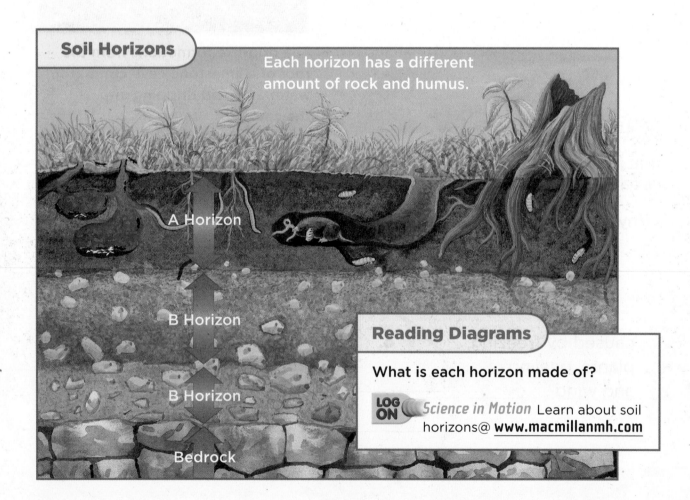

Soil Horizons

Each horizon has a different amount of rock and humus.

A Horizon

B Horizon

B Horizon

Bedrock

Reading Diagrams

What is each horizon made of?

LOG ON *Science in Motion* Learn about soil horizons@ **www.macmillanmh.com**

Here are the three horizons, top to bottom.

Horizon	Description
A Horizon	The A horizon is topsoil. This layer has plants and animals living in it. Plant roots grow down into it. Animals dig homes in it. It is rich in humus. There are few large rocks.
B Horizon	B horizon is the subsoil. Some plant roots may grow down into this layer. There is little humus. Broken pieces of rock are scattered through this layer.
C Horizon	This layer is made up largely of chunks of rock broken by weathering. There is also some rock that has not been broken. There are no plant roots or humus.

Beneath the horizons is *bedrock*. Bedrock is rock that has not been broken down or has only been partly broken down.

- Bedrock may be the same rock as in the layers above. OR
- The layers above the bedrock may have been carried there from another place and may have different rocks.

✓ Quick Check

Match the layers with the descriptions.

6. _____ A horizon   **a.** largely rocks broken by weathering

7. _____ B horizon   **b.** rock that is mostly not broken by weathering

8. _____ C horizon   **c.** rich in humus

9. _____ bedrock   **d.** very little humus and some plant roots

LOG ON **e-Review** Summaries and quizzes online @ www.macmillanmh.com

What causes erosion?

Rocks are slowly breaking down into smaller pieces all the time by weathering. The pieces of rock are then carried away by wind or by moving water. Carrying away broken pieces of rock is **erosion** (i•ROH•zhuhn).

Moving Water

Rivers and waves cause erosion. Small streams and large rivers pick up small pieces of rock as they flow downhill. They can carry the rock pieces for long distances and eventually drop them off.

Waves can break rocks apart in small pieces and sand. The waves can then carry the pieces to new places.

Waves carry sand, pebbles, and rocks and drop them off in new places.

Wind

Wind carries sand, soil, and small pieces of rock. At the same time, wind-driven sand can drill into rocks and wear them away.

Dropping Off Pieces of Rocks

Whenever moving water and wind slow down, they drop off some of pieces of rock they are carrying. Dropping off broken pieces of rock is **deposition** (dep•uh•ZISH•uhn).

Wind can drop off rocks just about anywhere. Rivers drop them off along the sides, or banks. Just about everything gets dropped off at the moth, or end, of a river.

This photo of the Mississippi was taken by a satellite way above the ground. The river is flowing into the Gulf of Mexico and drops off all that it carries. ▶

The Mississippi River

dropped off sand and rocks

The Gulf of Mexico

 Quick Check

Write a sentence about each of these words. Explain how one of these happens first and which happens later.

        erosion   deposition

10. _____

11. _____

What affects erosion?

Erosion goes faster when:

- the size of rock pieces and soil is small
- wind or moving water is fast and strong, as in floods or wind storms
- when there are no plants to hold the soil and pieces of rocks down. Plant roots hold soil together and slow up erosion.
- when soil is dry and sandy.

The Dust Bowl

During the 1920s soil was overused by many farmers. In the 1930s, there was almost no rain for almost 10 years. Crops would not grow. The dry, bare soil was carried away by winds causing the Dust Bowl.

Thick clouds of dust blew for miles. When the wind slowed down, the dust was dropped off onto farmland and homes.

The Dust Bowl

Northeast

West

Midwest

Dust Bowl

Southwest

Southeast

Reading Maps

The Dust Bowl happened in the brown part of the map, which includes some of the Midwest (the green states), Southwest (blue), and West (purple).

The Dust Bowl was the dry, bare area where clouds of sand and dust blew everywhere. Whenever the wind slowed down, sand and dust were dropped off and covered homes and farms. Thousands of farmers had to leave their farms.

Slowing Up Erosion

Today farmers can slow up erosion.

- They plant trees between fields to block the wind and hold the soil down.
- They plant crops in strips. One strip is a food crop. The next strip is a plant that holds soil down.
- They plow across a slope, not up and down a slope. This kind of plowing keeps water from rushing downhill and carrying soil away.

Strips of different crops are planted across a slope rather than up and down a slope.

✔ *Quick Check*

Fill in the missing "Effects" with

slow erosion or **fast erosion**

Cause		Effect
soil with plant roots	→	12. _____
strong winds	→	13. _____
plowing across a slope	→	14. _____
dry, sandy soil	→	15. _____

LOG ON e-**Review** Summaries and quizzes online @ **www.macmillanmh.com**

What is a landform?

If you traveled across North America, you would see many landforms. **Landforms** are the natural features on Earth's surface. They include:

- mountains, the tallest landforms
- hills, land rising above the surface but not as tall as mountains
- **plains**, wide, flat stretches of land without any hills or mountains
- winding rivers
- beaches
- deserts

Canyon Formation

Reading Photos

The winding river at the bottom of the canyon is still carving out the land, making it deeper and deeper.

Fast Changes, Slow Changes

Some landforms change quickly. For example, a mudslide can flow down a hill in minutes.

Most landforms such as a canyon, change slowly over many years. A **canyon** is a deep narrow landform with steep sides. Canyons often have rivers at the bottom.

A river drills into the land at the bottom of the canyon and breaks the rocks. The river then carries away the broken rocks. The bottom of the canyon becomes deeper and deeper.

▲ Homes in the Los Angeles, California area damaged by mudslides

✔ Quick Check

Complete the diagram. With just a few words in each box to sum up how canyons form.

| River flows in canyon | 16. _____ _____ _____ | 17. _____ _____ _____ |

Summary

The canyon gets deeper and deeper.

How can running water change land?

When it rains or when snow melts, water can:

- soak into the land
- run over the land.

Water that runs over the land flows downhill. As it flows, the water forms a pathway to the sea. That pathway is a river.

Down from the Mountains

High in the mountains water from rain or melted snow forms streams as it flows downhill. The streams come together and form larger rivers.

The rivers break up rocks along their sides. They carry the broken rocks away. As a result, rivers cause valleys to form. A **valley** is an area of low land between mountains. High in the mountains, valleys are deep with steep sides.

Mountain streams form rivers.
The rivers form valleys.

Rivers Curve

As a river flows down mountain, it reaches flatter land. The river slows down. Along one side of the river, moving water drops off some of the rocks it was carrying. The moving water wears away the other side of the river. By dropping off rocks on one side and wearing away the other, a river forms wide curves.

Into the Ocean

A river reaches its end, or mouth, when it flows into an ocean. At the mouth, a river drops off what it is carrying. The dropped off material forms a **delta** (DEL•tuh), an area of land at the mouth of a river.

Pieces of rock, soil, sand, and mud are dropped at the end of the river. The dropped-off material builds up into a delta.

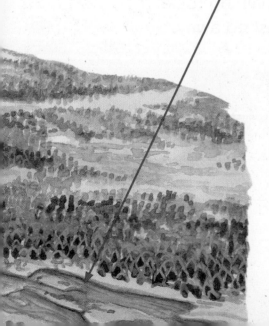

✓ **Quick Check**

Match the part of the river with the landform.

18. _____ curves   **a.** mouth

19. _____ delta   **b.** mountain

20. _____ deep valley   **c.** flat land

Wave action wore away a hole in this cliff in Cabo San Lucas, Mexico.

How can waves change land

As waves pound on a shore, they can cause beaches to change. Waves can pick up sand and move it to another part of a beach. Large waves in a storm can wash away a beach in hours.

Changing Rocky Cliffs

Waves can pound into the bottom of a rocky cliff. The bottom of the cliff slowly wears away. The top of the cliff eventually falls because there is little support underneath. The remaining rocks are broken into small pieces and washed away.

✅ Quick Check

21. What do you think will happen to the cliff in the photo as time

goes by? _____

_____

_____

Barrier Islands

Barrier islands are long, narrow strips of land built up from sand that was dropped along a shore. Barrier islands run along coasts. They protect coasts from being worn away by waves.

A barrier island changes shape all the time. Waves pick up sand from one part of the island and drop it on another part.

bay

coast

ocean

barrier island

◀ Barrier islands protect the coast of Long Island in New York.

 Quick Check

Fill in the boxes with ways waves can change the land.

Waves pick up and drop off sand	22. _____ _____ _____	23. _____ _____ _____

Summary

Waves change the land.

How can wind change land?

Wind carries sand and bits of rock. These wind-driven particles act like tiny drills. They can drill away softer parts of a large rock or even of a landform, like a hill. Over many years what remains of the landform is a rock with an unusual shape.

Wind can build sand dunes. **Sand dunes** are hills built from sand that is carried and dropped off by wind. When wind is blocked by a rock or a clump of grass, the wind drops off sand. Gradually a small hill builds up around the rock or clump of grass. Sand dunes can change shape as wind blows across them.

These smooth, low hills are sand dunes in Death Valley California.

Wind-driven sand drilled away at the softer parts of this rock and made this unusual shape. ▶

 Quick Check

Complete the sentence with two answers.

Wind changes the land by making

24. _____.

25. _____.

How can ice change land?

Many cold parts of Earth have glaciers (GLAY•shuhrz). **Glaciers** are large, thick sheets of ice. They can move slowly across the land by flowing downhill.

Over millions of years, glaciers have moved through valleys and across plains. They have crushed rocks and moved them along. As glaciers melt over time, they leave behind valleys with a wide, deep shape.

Hubbard glacier in Alaska is 122 kilometers (76 miles) long.

After a glacier moved through a valley, the valley has a U shape.

✔ Quick Check

Answer the question in complete sentences.

26. Why are glaciers able to change the shape of the land? _____

_____

_____

 e-Review Summaries and quizzes online @ www.macmillanmh.com

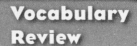

Slow Changes on Earth

Use a word from the box to name each example described below.

| physical weathering |
| chemical weathering |
| barrier island |
| sand dune |
| erosion |
| deposition |
| landform |

1. Ice forms in a crack in a rock and makes

the rock split. _____

2. Chemicals in the air mix with rocks and
eat away holes in them or make them

crumble. _____

3. long, narrow land that forms along a

coast or protects the coast _____

4. sand that is dropped by wind around a rock or clump

of grass _____

5. sand, soil, and pieces of rock carried away by moving

water and wind _____

6. sand, soil, and pieces of rock dropped off by moving

water or wind _____

7. hill, mountain, valley, or canyon _____

8. a layer of soil, such as topsoil or subsoil _____

Answer the question. Use at least one word from the box at the top of the page.

9. How can moving water change the land?

_____

_____

Read each clue. Write the answers in the blanks and then fill in the crossword puzzle.

Across

3. a large moving sheet of ice

5. a deep, narrow landform with steep sides, usually with a river running through it

6. breaking down rocks into small pieces

Down

1. the low land between hills or mountains

2. land built from rock pieces dropped off at the end of the river

4. a flat stretch of land without any hills or mountains

7. rotted plant and animal remains that becomes part of the soil

CHAPTER 5

Fast Changes on Earth

Vocabulary

 **landslide** the quick downhill movement of loose rocks and soil

 **plate** a large, moving piece of the crust

 **flood** large amount of water overflowing the sides of a river or a drain

 **fault** a crack in the crust

 **mudslide** water-soaked land that slides down a hill

 **earthquake** a sudden movement in the crust

What causes Earth's surface to change quickly?

volcano a mountain that builds up around an opening in the crust

hot spot a place in the crust where magma rises almost to the surface

hot spot

crust Earth's outermost layer

vent the opening in the center of a volcano

crater

crater a cuplike shape that forms around the vent of a volcano

tsunami a giant wave caused by an earthquake

How do landslides change the land quickly?

You may have seen skaters or skiers move down a hill. Loose rock and soil can move down a hill as well. They can move slowly, only centimeters a year. However they may also move quickly.

The quick downhill movement of loose rocks and soil is a **landslide**. In California landslides often occur in the mountains and along the coast.

Landslides happen when loose rocks are shaken, causing them to move downhill, such as by:

• an earthquake or erupting volcano
• storms with heavy rains
• building homes and offices in hilly areas
• the freezing of water in rocks, which can make them split.

This landslide in California was caused by the Loma Prieta earthquake in 1989. ▶

A landslide can move a huge amount of rocks and soil. As it moves it can carry along and bury homes and cars.

On the Lookout for Landslides

You can protect yourself from landslides:

- during heavy rains, listen to the TV or radio for landslide warnings
- learn the signs of a possible landslide: tilting of trees and poles, cracking sounds of trees, cracks in bottoms of buildings
- move away from the path of an oncoming landslide. If you can't, curl up into a tight ball to protect your head.

▲ Over 35 homes were damaged in the La Conchita landslide in January of 2005.

✔ Quick Check

What are two causes of a landslide? What is an effect of landslides? Fill your answers in the diagram.

Cause	→	Effect
1. _____	→	landslide
2. _____	→	landslide
landslide	→	3. _____

How do floods change the land quickly?

In any rainfall, some water soaks into the ground and some flows across the land. In a heavy rainfall, water may not soak into the ground fast enough. As a result, a very large amount of water can flow across the land.

The flowing water may spill into a river or drain. A large amount of water overflowing the sides of a river or a drain is a **flood**.

Effects of Floods

The large amount of water and its fast speed can cause much damage:

- floods can damage cars and buildings
- floods can wash away bridges
- floods can carry away soil from farmland
- floods can carry soil and mud and drop them onto homes, streets, and cars.

▲ Flooding of the Mississippi River in the early 1990s caused billions of dollars of damage.

Floods and Mudslides

Heavy rain and floods may soak into the land on a hill and cause a mudslide. A **mudslide** is water-soaked land that slides downhill. The flowing mud can bury homes and cars. The mud blocks floodwater from draining away.

On the Lookout for Floods

During heavy rains, listen to the local weather reports for *flood watches* and *flood warnings*.

- A flood watch means flooding is possible. Get ready to leave in case you are told to do so.
- A flood warning means that a flood is occurring or will occur soon. You will have to move to higher ground.

This car in San Bernardino was buried by a mudslide in 2003.

✓ Quick Check

Fill in the missing "Cause" or "Effect" in each row of the diagram.

Cause	→	Effect
4. _____	→	flood
flood	→	5. _____
6. _____	→	mudslide

LOG ON **e-Review** Summaries and quizzes online @ **www.macmillanmh.com**

What are earthquakes?

Earth's surface is always changing. Most changes are slow, such as weathering. Sometimes changes happen quickly. For example, Earth's surface can shake or shift suddenly.

Earth's Moving Crust

Earth's surface is covered with its crust. The **crust** is Earth's outermost layer, much like an apple has an outer layer of skin. The crust is made up of all of Earth's land, including the ocean bottoms.

The crust is broken into huge pieces, or **plates**. The plates fit together like puzzle pieces. Unlike puzzle pieces, the plates can move.

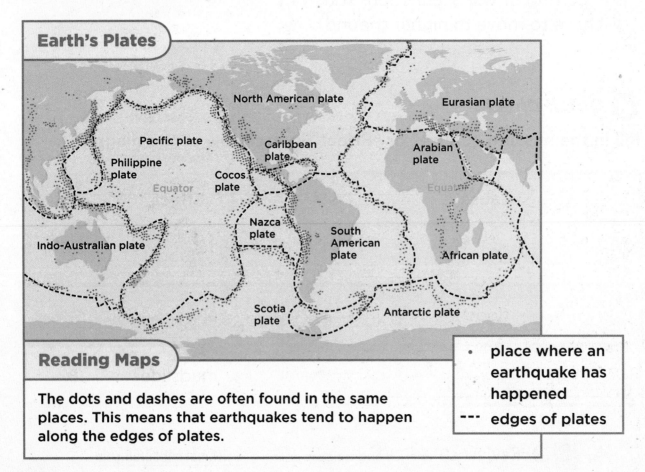

Earth's Plates

North American plate

Eurasian plate

Pacific plate

Caribbean plate

Arabian plate

Philippine plate

Cocos plate

Equator

Equator

Nazca plate

Indo-Australian plate

South American plate

African plate

Scotia plate

Antarctic plate

Reading Maps

The dots and dashes are often found in the same places. This means that earthquakes tend to happen along the edges of plates.

- place where an earthquake has happened
- - - edges of plates

▲ Route 14 near Sylmar, California, was heavily damaged as a result of an earthquake on January 17, 1994.

At the edges of the plates, there are cracks in the crust. These cracks are called **faults**. Along a fault, two plates can move by:

- sliding past each other
- pushing into each other
- pulling apart.

When plates move, earthquakes can happen. An **earthquake** is a movement in the crust caused by a sudden shift of the plates.

As the red dots in the map show, earthquakes tend to happen at the edges of the plates. Most earthquakes happen around the Pacific Ocean.

Quick Check

Match the description with the word.

7. _____ happens at plate edges   **a.** crust

8. _____ piece of the crust   **b.** earthquake

9. _____ crack in the crust   **c.** plate

10. _____ all of Earth's land   **d.** fault

What causes an earthquake?

Earthquakes happen along cracks, or faults, in the crust. Along a fault, parts of the crust on either side may:

• rise up or move down
• slide past each other.

The movement may be very slow, just centimeters a year. In that case, an earthquake does not happen. Instead, when parts of the crust move up or down *slowly* over many years, mountains may be formed.

When the movement is sudden, an earthquake happens. The ground shakes, or vibrates. The ground may split open. The ground vibrates in all directions from the center of the earthquake. People far from the center of the earthquake may feel a slight shaking.

Strike-Slip Fault

The plates slide past each other along the fault.

Reverse Fault

The plates push into each other. The part of the crust above the fault surface (in this case, the right side) rises up.

Normal Fault

The plates pull apart. The part of the crust above the fault surface (in this case, the right side) moves down.

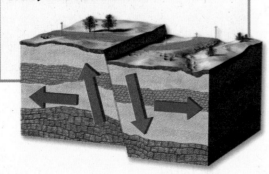

Earthquake Safety

People who live where earthquakes happen can stay safe. Here are some safety tips:

- Place breakable or heavy objects on lower shelves. Bolt down appliances. These are two ways to keep heavy objects from falling.
- Locate *safe spots* at home and school—such as under a sturdy table.
- If outside in a quake, move to an open space away from buildings or power lines. This way you can stay safe from things falling on you.
- Have family earthquake drills. Together find a safe spot. Then drop, cover, and hold on. Arrange a meeting place outside the home.
- Drivers should stop during an earthquake. Passengers should stay inside the car.

The Sierra Nevada mountains formed over centuries where plates pull apart.

Along the San Andreas Fault, rocks slide past each other. Many earthquakes in California take place along this fault.

 Quick Check

Fill in the missing "Effects" with slow erosion ➡ or ⬅ fast erosion.

Cause	⟶	Effect
sudden movement along a fault ⟶		**11.** _____
12. _____	⟶	Mountains may form.
Bolt appliances down. ⟶		**13.** _____
Move away from tall buildings. ⟶		**14.** _____

What is a tsunami?

Have you ever seen small waves rise and fall as they reach a shore. However, some large ocean waves can be 30 meters (100 feet) tall and travel at a speed of 960 kilometers (600 miles) per hour. That kind of a wave is a tsunami (sew•NAH•mee). **Tsunami** is a giant ocean wave.

Tsunamis are caused by:

- underwater landslides
- underwater erupting volcanoes
- most often, underwater earthquakes.

An earthquake may be strong enough to set a wave moving. In deep water the wave may pass by unnoticed. Closer to the shore, the wave slows down, but gets taller.

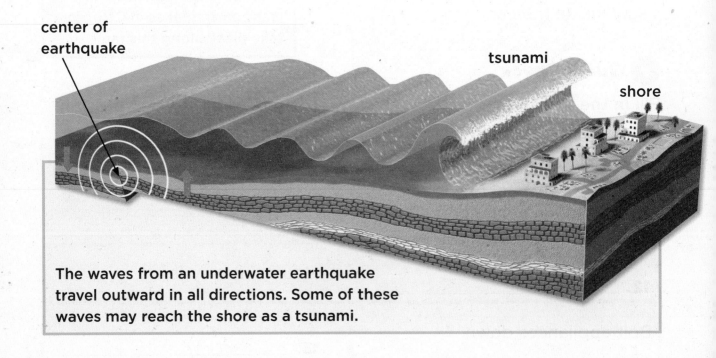

center of earthquake

tsunami

shore

The waves from an underwater earthquake travel outward in all directions. Some of these waves may reach the shore as a tsunami.

A tsunami may reach the shore as one huge wall of water or as several smaller waves. Either way, they are fast and powerful. They wash away beaches, property, and lives.

In December 2004, an earthquake in the Indian Ocean caused a tsunami to hit Sumatra. Then tsunamis reached Sri Lanka in two hours and South Africa in seven hours—800 kilometers (5,000 miles) from the earthquake.

If you are near a coast and learn of an earthquake, listen to news reports for tsunami warnings. If there is a warning, move to higher ground immediately.

Nearly 300,000 people lost their lives in the tsunami of December 2004, mostly in Sumatra.

✔ Quick Check

15. What are some ways a tsunami can form?

_____

16. Why are tsunamis dangerous?

_____

LOG ON **e-Review** Summaries and quizzes online @ **www.macmillanmh.com**

What is a volcano?

Did you ever shake a can of soda and then open it. Shaking releases gas from the soda. The gas explodes in a spray. Something similar can happen to a volcano.

A **volcano** is a mountain built up around an opening in the crust. The opening may form from a crack. Sometimes magma may melt upward and crack the land. In either case, a volcano may *erupt* suddenly—forcing out melted rock, gases, and pieces of solid rock.

A volcano erupts when magma (melted rock) below the volcano rises to the surface. Gases escape from the magma as it rises. If the gases escape slowly, a volcano erupts gently. If the gases escape quickly, a volcano explodes.

▲ When Mount St. Helens erupted in 1980, it "blew its top," leaving a huge cuplike opening at the top. The land around the volcano was buried under ash and soot.

Rising Magma

At the center of a volcano is an opening called a **vent**. The vent may form from movement along a fault. Or magma may melt upward and crack through the surface.

As magma rises up through a vent, it reaches the surface. When magma reaches the surface, it becomes *lava*. Lava is melted rock that starts to cool and harden.

Lava can ooze or explode out of a volcano. Either way, it hardens into a layer around the vent. Some volcanoes release ash, which also forms a layer. The volcano gets bigger each time the volcano erupts and lava and ash build up around the vent.

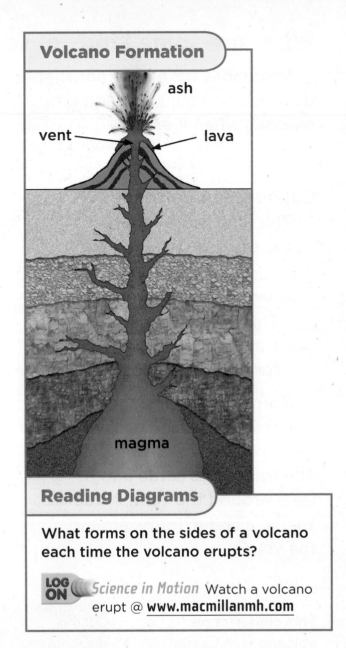

Volcano Formation

ash

vent

lava

magma

Reading Diagrams

What forms on the sides of a volcano each time the volcano erupts?

LOG ON *Science in Motion* Watch a volcano erupt @ **www.macmillanmh.com**

 Quick Check

Fill in the boxes to explain how a volcano can erupt.

First **17.** _____

↓

Next **18.** _____

↓

Last The volcano erupts. Lava or ash is released.

What are some kinds of volcanoes?

Volcanoes have different shapes. The shape depends on how a volcano erupts and what it releases when it erupts.

Cinder-Cone Volcano

This kind of volcano:

- is shaped like a cone and has steep sides
- has thick magma inside. This magma has lots of trapped gas.
- forms from explosions.

With each explosion, lava bursts into the air. The lava hardens into rock fragments, The fragments settle into a layer around the vent. A cuplike shape, a **crater**, forms around the vent.

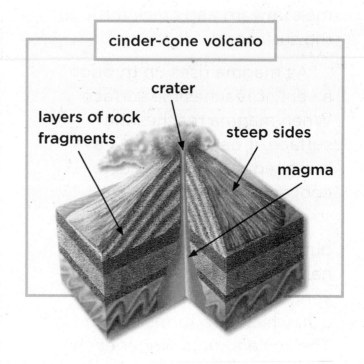

cinder-cone volcano

crater

layers of rock fragments

steep sides

magma

This cinder-cone volcano is in Lassen Volcanic National Park in northeastern California. ▶

Shield Volcano

This kind of volcano:

- has wide, almost flat sides
- forms from lava flowing from one or more openings.

This kind of volcano forms from layers of lava that build up over years. The Hawaiian Islands are all shield volcanoes.

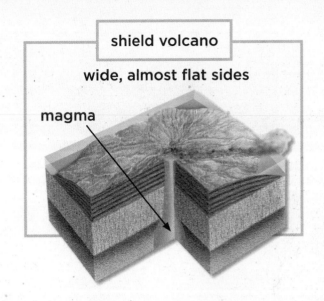

shield volcano

wide, almost flat sides

magma

Composite Volcano

This kind of volcano:

- is made up of layers of lava and ash
- has a cone shape with sides that match, one as steep as another.

This kind of volcano forms when it erupts in two ways. It erupts quietly releasing lava. Then it explodes releasing ash. These two ways keep "taking turns."

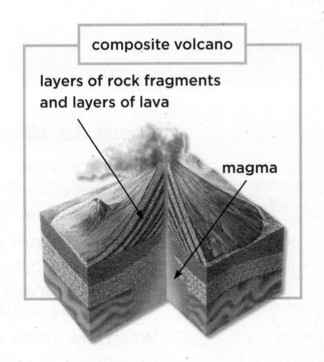

composite volcano

layers of rock fragments and layers of lava

magma

✔ Quick Check

Match the volcano with the description.

19. _____ cinder-cone

20. _____ shield

21. _____ composite

a. wide, almost flat sides

b. forms from lava and ash

c. forms from rock fragments

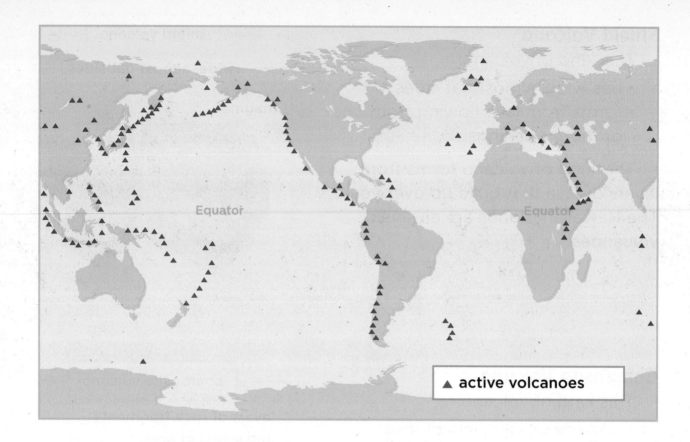

▲ active volcanoes

Where do volcanoes form?

Many volcanoes form at the edges of plates. Remember, plates are pieces of the crust. Volcanoes form where two plates meet.

- **When two plates push together** One plate moves under the other. The plate that moves down under melts and forms magma. The magma rises and forms a volcano

- **When two plates pull apart** Magma rises up through an opening when plates pull apart. These volcanoes often form along the ocean bottom.

- **Hot spots** Some volcanoes form in the middle of a plate. They form when a plate moves over a hot spot. A **hot spot** is a place where magma has melted part of the way through the crust.

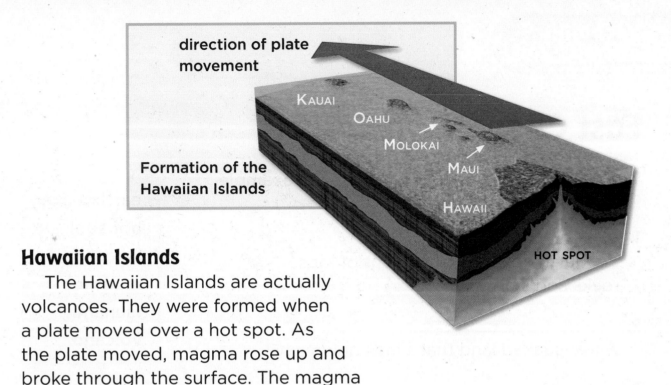

direction of plate movement

KAUAI

OAHU

MOLOKAI

MAUI

HAWAII

Formation of the Hawaiian Islands

HOT SPOT

Hawaiian Islands

The Hawaiian Islands are actually volcanoes. They were formed when a plate moved over a hot spot. As the plate moved, magma rose up and broke through the surface. The magma formed one volcano after another in a chain. Hawaii is the youngest island, the only one still erupting.

Volcano Safety

To stay safe where volcanoes may erupt:

- stay away from lava flows
- have breathing masks and goggles ready
- obey your town's warning system. Leave immediately if told to do so.

✓ Quick Check

How do volcanoes form at each place?

22. where two plates push together _____

23. hot spot _____

24. Why are breathing masks important if you live near an active

volcano? _____

LOG ON **e-Review** Summaries and quizzes online @ **www.macmillanmh.com**

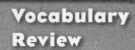

Fast Changes on Earth

Use a word from the box to name each example
described below.

earthquake
hot spot
landslide
mudslide
tsunami
volcano

1. _____

the quick downhill movement of loose
rocks and soil

2. _____

water-soaked land that slides down a hill

3. _____

a sudden movement in the crust

4. _____

a giant wave caused by an earthquake

5. _____

a mountain that builds up around an opening in Earth's crust

6. _____

a place in the crust where magma rises almost to the surface

**Answer the question. Use at least one word from the box at the
top of the page.**

7. How can moving water change the land? _____

_____

Write the missing words in the blanks. Then find the same words in the puzzle.

1. A cuplike shape that forms around the vent of a volcano

_____.

2. Earth's outermost layer _____.

3. A crack in Earth's crust _____.

4. Large amount of water overflowing the sides of a river or a drain

_____.

5. A large, moving piece of Earth's crust _____.

6. the opening in the center of a volcano _____.

```
O  M  D  O  H  G  I  V  B  J  T  U  I  G  Y
Y  E  X  S  P  S  D  O  W  Z  S  I  H  Z  Y
W  W  X  G  Y  S  I  I  V  D  U  C  I  E  G
N  V  P  E  F  L  T  E  H  R  R  H  G  G  G
H  E  W  O  B  H  U  G  S  A  C  N  K  Q  E
L  T  K  S  B  V  U  Y  D  F  A  U  L  T  U
Q  N  K  N  L  J  I  V  M  O  H  U  A  Q  G
K  N  I  P  C  H  Q  C  E  S  O  L  S  A  K
V  N  N  J  V  B  N  X  T  N  P  L  W  P  L
R  E  T  A  R  C  E  U  P  L  T  N  F  B  C
F  P  U  A  B  J  T  N  O  Y  E  F  D  V  B
I  W  M  O  P  S  B  V  C  P  K  U  H  F  L
K  L  R  M  H  J  T  C  B  E  B  G  R  M  T
I  J  Y  G  V  F  N  J  C  V  T  R  G  G  T
Z  Q  I  M  I  B  W  Q  W  V  Q  H  I  Q  D
```

CHAPTER 6

Electricity

Vocabulary

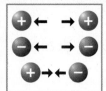 **electrical charge** one of two kinds of particles, positive or negative, that are in objects

 **static electricity** a build up of electrical charges on an object

 **discharge** a sudden movement of electrical charges from one object to another

 **conductor** a material that lets electric charges flow through it easily

 **insulator** a material that does not let electric charges flow through it easily

 **electric current** a flow of electrical charges through a material, such as a wire

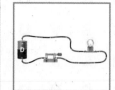 **circuit** the path of an electric current

How do we use electricity?

 voltage a measure of how strong a battery or any other power source is

 **series circuit** a circuit in which the electrical charges flow through a single path

 **parallel circuit** a circuit in which the electrical charges flow through more than one path

 **transformer** an electrical tool that increases or decreases the voltage in an electric current

 **circuit breaker** an electrical tool that switches off an electric current that gets too high

 **fuse** an electrical tool that melts to open a circuit if the electric current gets too high

What is electrical charge?

What is electricity? To answer the question, you need to think that everything is made up of tiny particles, too small to be seen.

Each of these tiny particles can have an electrical charge. There are two kinds of **electrical charge**, positive or negative, that can:

- repel (push away) each other—if they are the same kind of charge
- attract (pull toward) each other, if they are opposite charges.

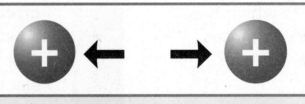

two positive charges repel each other

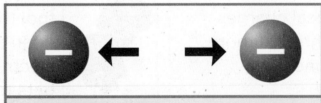

two negative charges repel each other

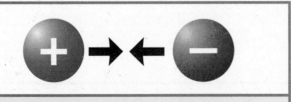

opposite charges attract each other

Charges Add Up

Most objects are made up of the same number of positive and negative charges. Objects with the same number of both charges are neutral (NEW•truhl).

When two objects touch or nearly touch, charged particles can move from one object to the other. Negative charges move from object to object more easily than positive charges.

For example, rub a balloon with a wool cloth:
- negative charges move from the wool to the balloon
- the balloon now has more negative charges than positive charges. The balloon is negatively charged.

▲ Charged particles in the girl's hair are attracted to the charged balloon.

✓ Quick Check

Fill in each empty particle with a "+" or "-" to show if the two particles attract or repel.

1.

2.

Draw arrows in between these particles to show if these two are attracting or repelling.

3.

What is static electricity?

A balloon starts out with the same number of positive charges and negative charges. Remember what happens if you rub the balloon with a wool cloth? Negative charges move from the wool to the balloon.

Rubbing causes a *buildup* of negative charges on the balloon. A buildup means that there are now more negative charges on the balloon than positive charges. The balloon is negatively charged. A buildup of electrical charges on an object is called **static electricity**.

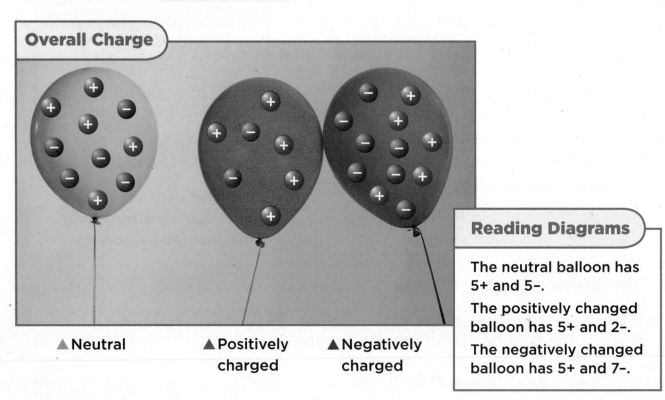

Overall Charge

▲ Neutral   ▲ Positively charged   ▲ Negatively charged

Reading Diagrams

The neutral balloon has 5+ and 5–.

The positively changed balloon has 5+ and 2–.

The negatively changed balloon has 5+ and 7–.

✔ Quick Check

4. Why are the two balloons in the diagram attracting?

_____

_____

_____

As you saw, rubbing can cause negative charges to move from one object (such as wool) to another (a balloon). Charged particles can also move *inside* an object.

Think of what happens when you try this:

- Rub a balloon with wool. Rubbing causes a buildup of negative charges on the balloon.
- Hold the negatively charged balloon near a wall. Positive charges in the wall are attracted to the balloon and move toward it. Negative charges in the wall are repelled from the balloon and move away.
- The wall and the balloon attract each other. The balloon sticks to the wall.

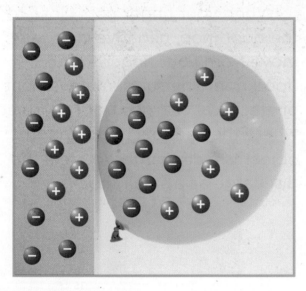

◀ The balloon is negatively charged. The wall is neutral, but the positive charges build up in the wall near the balloon.

Quick Check

Complete the Main Idea diagram. List two details that help explain the main idea.

Main Idea	Details
The balloon sticks to the wall.	5. _____ 6. _____

What is an electrical discharge?

Follow this sequence of events:

1. You walk across a carpet, dragging your feet.

2. Negative charges move from the carpet and build up on your body. You become negatively charged.

3. You reach out to touch a metal doorknob to open a door. OUCH!

When your finger gets close to the doorknob, negative charges move from your finger to the doorknob. The sudden movement of electrical charges from an object where they are built up to another object is a **discharge**. You feel the discharge as a small shock.

▲ You feel the discharge as a shock. If the room is dark enough, you would see a tiny flash of light.

Quick Check

Correct each of these false sentences.

7. You become positively charged when you walk across a rug. _____

_____

8. You feel a shock when negative particles move from the doorknob to your hand. _____

_____

What conductors and insulators?

How can you avoid getting a shock from touching a metal doorknob? Touch the wooden door first. Why?

The metal is a conductor. A **conductor** is a material that lets charges flow through it easily. Charges race to the metal doorknob and flow into it. You feel a shock.

Metals such as copper and silver are good conductors. Even a person can be a conductor. That's why you can get a shock when another person touches you.

Wood is an insulator. An **insulator** is a material that does not let charges flow through it easily. When you touch a wooden door, charges move slowly onto the door. You don't feel a shock. Other insulators are:

- glass
- rubber
- plastic

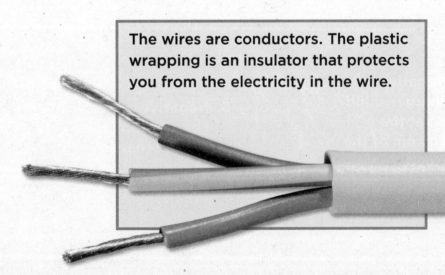

The wires are conductors. The plastic wrapping is an insulator that protects you from the electricity in the wire.

 Quick Check

In each row cross out the word or words that do not belong.

9. insulator   glass   copper   silver   lets charges flow

10. insulator   plastic   rubber   does not let charges flow

What is lightning?

Lightning is a discharge of static electricity between:

- a cloud and the ground
- two clouds
- two oppositely charged parts of a cloud.

To help you understand how lightning forms, remember that charges can move *inside* something. Charges can move to different parts of a cloud and the ground. Now follow the numbers in the diagram to see how lightning occurs between a cloud and the ground.

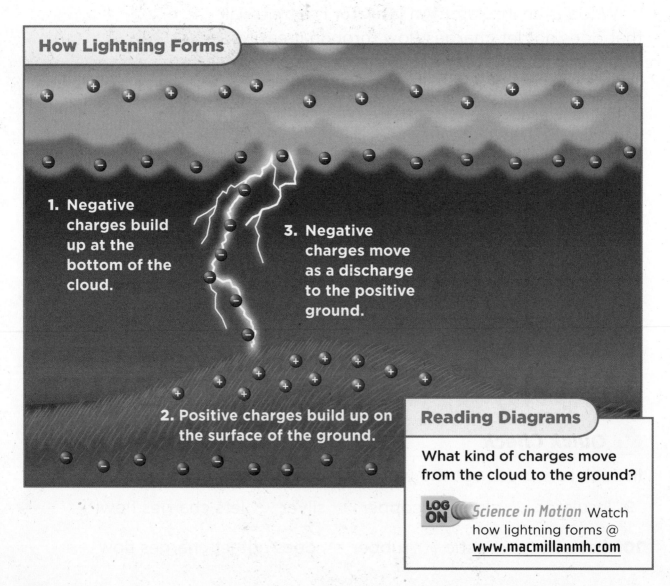

How Lightning Forms

1. Negative charges build up at the bottom of the cloud.

3. Negative charges move as a discharge to the positive ground.

2. Positive charges build up on the surface of the ground.

Reading Diagrams

What kind of charges move from the cloud to the ground?

LOG ON *Science in Motion* Watch how lightning forms @ **www.macmillanmh.com**

Lightning Safety

Lightning takes the shortest path to the ground. It hits the tallest object or best conductor.

If you hear thunder or see lightning, follow these rules to stay safe:

 Lightning Safety

1. Find shelter inside a building, a car, or truck. Do not seek shelter under a tree.

2. If you are far from any shelter, then go to the lowest point and squat or lay down. You do not want to be the tallest object in the area.

3. If you are in the water (such as a pool, the ocean, or a lake), get out of the water immediately. Lightning often strikes bodies of water.

 Quick Check

11. What causes lightning to form between the cloud and the ground?

_____

_____

Fill in the Main Idea diagram. List two details that support the main idea.

Main Idea	Details
You can be safe when there is lightning.	**12.** _____
	13. _____

LOG ON **e-Review** Summaries and quizzes online @ **www.macmillanmh.com**

What is electric current?

When you plug in a TV set and turn it on, electric charges are flowing through wires. A flow of electric charges is an **electric current**. In an electric current, electric charges keep moving until you turn the current off.

Circuits

An electric current needs a path to carry the charges. The path an electric current follows is a **circuit**. A circuit has several parts:

- a power source—such as a battery
- a load—something that uses electricity to work such as a lamp, a TV, or a computer
- wires and other things that connect the parts

Many circuits also have a switch. A switch is used to turn the electric current on or off. The circuit shown here has all the parts, So why do you think the bulb is not lit up? The switch is up.

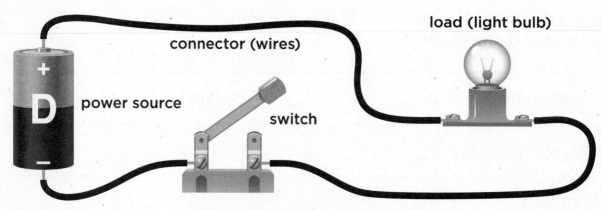

load (light bulb)

connector (wires)

power source

switch

▲ The switch in this circuit is up, so that the circuit has a break in it. Electric current cannot flow.

Open and Closed Circuit

When the switch is up, the circuit is open. An *open circuit* has a break or opening. Electric current cannot flow in an open circuit. Circuits are open if a bulb burns out or if wires are loose.

The switch is closed in the circuit below. Current flows because there are no breaks in the circuit. A complete, unbroken circuit is a *closed circuit*.

Every circuit needs a power source, something that moves the electrical current. The power source shown here is a battery. Any power source has a certain amount of voltage (VOHL•tij). **Voltage** is the strength of a power source with greater voltage, more electric current can flow.

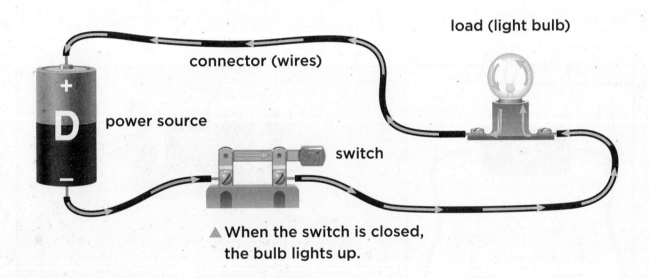

load (light bulb)

connector (wires)

power source

switch

▲ When the switch is closed, the bulb lights up.

✔ Quick Check

Match the description with the word.

14. _____ something that uses electricity

15. _____ a flow of electric charges

16. _____ a path for the electric charges

17. _____ the strength of a battery

a. circuit

b. voltage

c. load

d. electric current

What is a series circuit?

What are the parts of the circuit shown in the diagram and the photograph? Start with a battery. There are two bulbs. A wire is used to connect the battery and the bulbs.

This simple circuit does not need a switch. As soon as all the parts are connected, the circuit is closed. Electric current flows and both bulbs light up.

This is a series (SEER•eez) circuit. In a **series circuit**, all the electrical charges flow in one direction along a single path. There is only one way for the electric current to go.

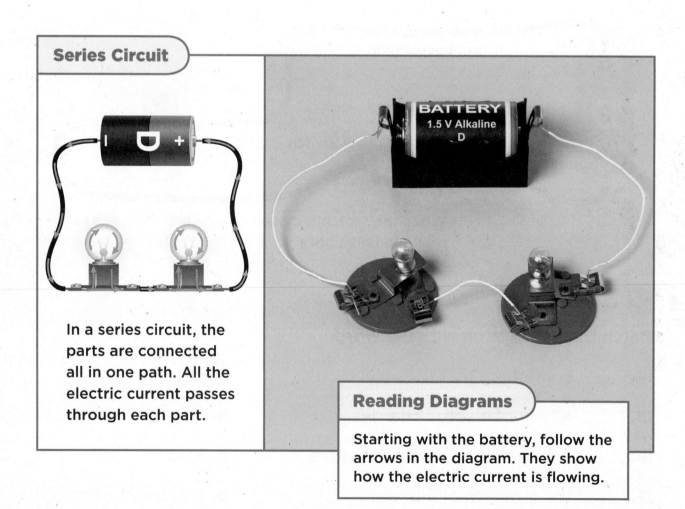

Series Circuit

In a series circuit, the parts are connected all in one path. All the electric current passes through each part.

Reading Diagrams

Starting with the battery, follow the arrows in the diagram. They show how the electric current is flowing.

If any part of a series circuit is removed, the circuit is open. None of the parts will work because the electric current stops flowing.

For example, the electric current stops if one bulb burns out or is removed from the circuit. Because the electric current stops, the other bulb no longer lights up.

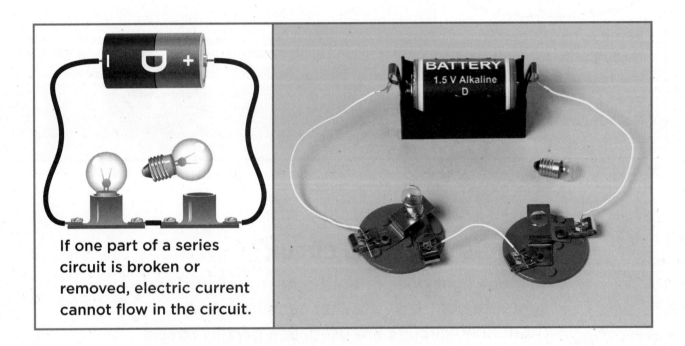

If one part of a series circuit is broken or removed, electric current cannot flow in the circuit.

✔ Quick Check

Complete the diagram below.

Cause →	Effect
Connect all the parts of this series circuit. →	**18.** _____
Remove one bulb from the circuit. →	**19.** _____

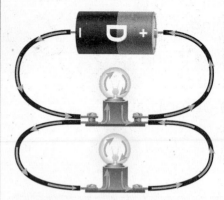

Some current flows through the top path and the rest of the current goes to the bottom path. Both bulbs light up.

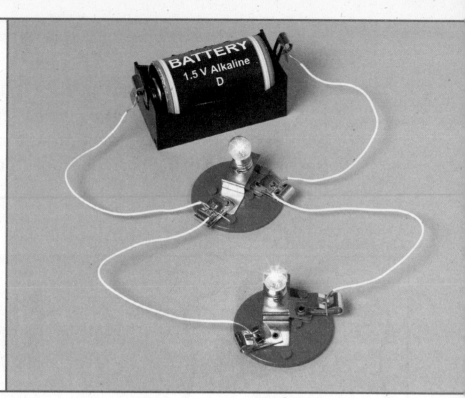

What is a parallel circuit?

If one light goes out at home, the rest of the lights stay on. They stay on because parallel (PA•ruh•lel) circuits are used. In a **parallel circuit**, electric current flows through more than one path.

The pictures here show how a parallel circuit works. The parts are the same as the parts in a series circuit. However, the parts are connected so that there are two paths for the electric current

In a parallel circuit, some of the electric current flows through one path. Some flows through another path. In bigger circuits, there may be many more than just two paths.

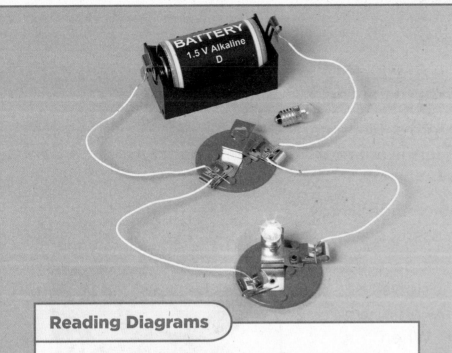

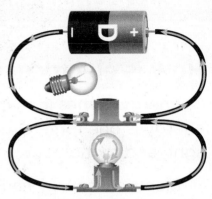

If the bulb from the top path is removed, the electric current can pass by the break in the circuit. It can light up the bottom bulb.

Reading Diagrams

Follow the arrows from the "-" side of the battery. The arrows show how the current can pass by the break in the top path and flow to the bottom path.

If any path of a parallel circuit is opened, the current still flows through the other paths. So if a light bulb in one path is removed or burns out, other bulbs in other paths can still stay lit.

One danger is that all the electric current may flow through one very short path, a *short circuit*. The result can be overheated wires and a fire.

✅ *Quick Check*

20. How can you tell a parallel circuit from a series circuit? _____

_____

21. Why is a parallel circuit helpful at home? _____

_____

How is electrical energy used?

Energy comes in many forms. Electrical energy is one form. Other forms are heat, light, and motion.

Electrical energy can be changed into other forms all the time in useful ways.

- **heat** When electric current passes through very thin wires, it slows down—much like cars slowing down when a road gets narrow. When electric current slows down, the wires get hot. Burners, heaters, hair dryers, and toasters produce heat by using certain wires that cause electric current to slow down.
- **light** When electric current flows through thin wires, the wires can get hot enough to glow. That is how some light bulbs work.
- **motion** Electric motors change electric current to motion. Motors run trains, washing machines, and cars.

▲ The wires in a burner slow down electric current so much that the burner gets hot and glows.

✔ Quick Check

For each device, tell what change of energy takes place.

22. car _____

23. hair dryer _____

23. bulb _____

How can we use electricity safely?

Here are two tips for using electricity safely:

- **bared wires** Be sure the coating around a wire is unbroken. The coating is an insulator. If the coating tears and the wire is bared, the wire can touch another wire. A short circuit can heat the wire and start a fire.
- **overloaded outlets** Never plug too many devices into one outlet. They can overheat circuits in the wall and start a fire.

Homes and buildings are protected against overheating wires. Circuits are protected by:

- **circuit breakers**, which switch open a circuit if the current gets too high.
- **fuses**, which melt, causing a circuit to open if the current gets too high.

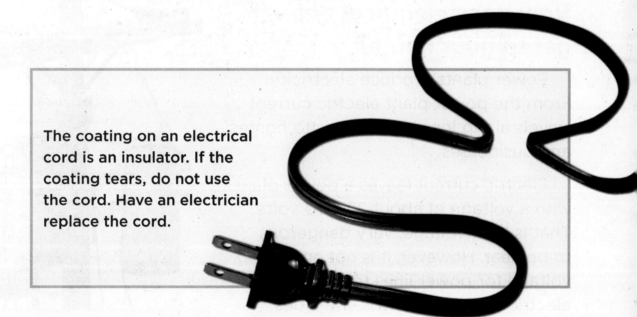

The coating on an electrical cord is an insulator. If the coating tears, do not use the cord. Have an electrician replace the cord.

 Quick Check

25. To use electricity safely at home, look out for _____

_____

▲ Power lines carry electric current at a very high voltage. They are covered with an insulator, but you must still keep away to be safe.

How does electrical energy get to your home?

Power plants produce electricity. From the power plant electric current travels along long power lines to homes and businesses.

Electric current leaves a power plant with a voltage of about 25,000 volts. That is high voltage, very dangerous to be near. However, it is not enough voltage for power lines to carry the electric current to towns and cities.

An electric tool called a **transformer** can change the voltage. Electric current from the power plant enters a transformer. The transformer increases the voltage to about 400,000 volts!

Before reaching your home, electric current goes through a transformer like this one. This transformer decreases voltage.

The Path of Energy

① Electrical energy is produced at a power plant.

② A transformer increases voltage of the electric current.

③ A transformer lowers the voltage of current.

④ Another transformer lowers the voltage so it is safe enough to enter a home.

⑤ Electrical cables carry the electric current back to the power plant.

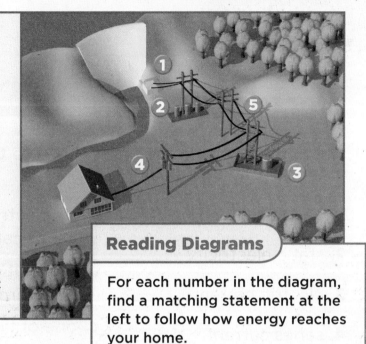

Reading Diagrams

For each number in the diagram, find a matching statement at the left to follow how energy reaches your home.

Before electric current reaches your home, it goes through other transformers. These transformers lower the voltage to safe levels. Most homes run on 120 volts or 240 volts.

Then current travels through different power lines back to the power plant. Transformers increase the voltage for the "trip."

✔ Quick Check

Tell how electric current gets to your home.

First Electricity is produced by a power plant.

⬇

Next 17. Transformers _____

⬇

Last 18. Transformers _____

LOG ON **e-Review** Summaries and quizzes online @ www.macmillanmh.com

Electricity

Match the words in the first column to the best answer in the second column.

1. electrical charge _____

2. static electricity _____

3. electric current _____

4. series current _____

5. parallel current _____

6. circuit breaker _____

a. an electrical tool that switches off an electrical current that gets too high

b. a circuit in which the electrical charges flow through more than one path

c. one of two kinds of particles in objects, positive or negative, that can cause objects to pull toward each other together or push away from each other

d. a flow of electrical charges through a material, such as a wire

e. a buildup of electrical charges on an object

f. circuit in which the electrical charges flow through a single path

Answer the following questions. Use one or more words from the first column above in each answer.

7. What happens when you rub a balloon with

a wool cloth? _____

_____

8. Each of two circuits has two bulbs. You remove a bulb from each circuit. In one circuit the remaining bulb goes out, but in the other circuit

it stays lit. What's the difference? _____

_____

Use the clues to fill in the crossword puzzle below.

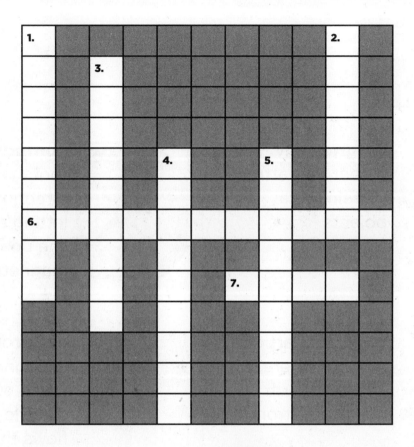

ACROSS

6. An electrical tool that increases or decreases the voltage in an electrical current

7. An electrical tool that melts to open a circuit if the electrical current gets too high

DOWN

1. A material that lets electric charges flow through it easily

2. A measure of how strong a battery or any other power source is

3. A material that does not let electric charges flow through it easily

4. A sudden movement of electrical charges from one object to another

5. The path of an electric current

CHAPTER 7

Magnetism

Vocabulary

magnet any object that attracts certain metal objects

compass a tool that shows directions by letting a needle line up with Earth's magnetic field

pole the part of a magnet where the ability to push or pull is the strongest

electromagnet a magnet that is made when an electric current flows through a coiled wire around an iron rod

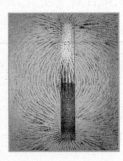

magnetic field the area around a magnet where it can push or pull another magnet

loudspeaker a tool that changes electrical energy into sound

How do we use magnets?

microphone a tool that changes sound into electric signals

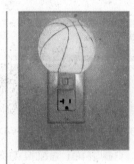

alternating current electrical current that flows in one direction and then in the opposite direction, back and forth

motor a tool that changes electrical energy into energy of motion

direct current electrical current that flows in just one direction

generator a tool that changes energy of motion into electrical energy

What is a magnet?

You may have used magnets to pull (or attract) things made of metal, like steel paper clips. A **magnet** is any object that attracts certain metal objects. A magnet also can attract or can push away (repel) another magnet.

Refrigerator Magnets

Refrigerator magnets are made up of very tiny strips of magnets placed next to each other. The way they are arranged causes the ability to attract to be very strong on one side of the magnet. That is why one side of the magnet attracts (or sticks to) the metal in a refrigerator.

Magnets come in many shapes—bars, circles, and this horseshoe shape. They attract metallic paper clips, but not plastic paper clips.

Magnetic Poles

Hold two bar magnets by strings. Point the ends toward each other. The ends will push or pull each other. The ends of a bar magnet are its poles. A **pole** is the part of a magnet where the ability to push or pull is the strongest.

Magnets have two poles—north (N) and south (S). When the poles are brought together:

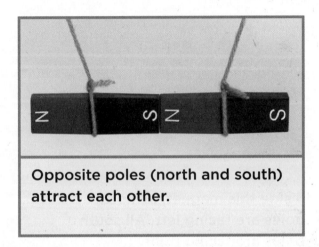

Opposite poles (north and south) attract each other.

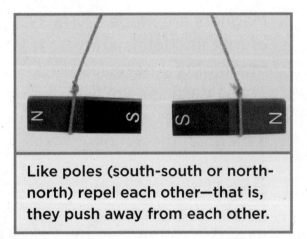

Like poles (south-south or north-north) repel each other—that is, they push away from each other.

The ability to attract or repel depends on how far apart two magnets are. The farther apart two magnets are, the weaker their ability to attract or repel each other becomes. Far enough apart, the magnets do not attract or repel at all.

 Quick Check

Fill in each space with an N or S to show that the two bar magnets attract or repel.

1. repel

2. attract

How do magnets attract?

Magnets attract some metal objects, like metal paper clips. How do magnets attract metals? When you bring a magnet near some metal objects, the metal objects actually become magnets. Here's how:

1. Magnets are made of metals. Metals are made of tiny particles. These particles are like tiny magnets. Inside a magnet, these tiny magnetic particles are all lined up. All the north poles face one direction. All the south poles face the other.

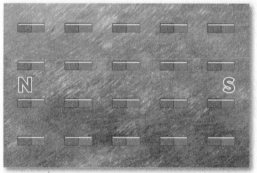

Inside this magnet, all north poles are facing left. All south poles are facing right.

2. Magnets attract certain metals, such as iron, nickel, and cobalt. If a metal is not a magnet, the metal still has tiny magnetic particles inside. However, they are not lined up. North poles and south poles are facing many different directions.

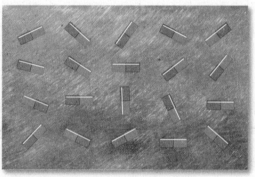

This piece of metal is NOT a magnet. The tiny particles inside are facing many directions.

3. Bring a bar magnet or any other permanent magnet near a piece of iron, nickel, or cobalt. The tiny magnetic particles turn around and line up. The metal becomes a temporary magnet. This temporary magnet attracts the bar magnet.

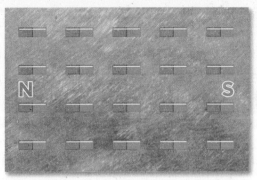

This piece of metal becomes a temporary magnet when you bring a permanent magnet near to it. All particles become lined up.

4. Take the permanent magnet away from the piece of metal. Usually, the tiny particles move around and face many directions again.

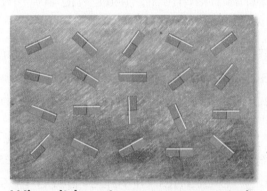

When it is not near a permanent magnet, the piece of metal no longer has particles all lined up.

✔ Quick Check

Fill in this diagram to show what happens when you bring a bar magnet next to a piece of iron.

3. First In a piece of iron, the tiny particles are

_____

↓

Next Bring a bar magnet near the piece of iron.

↓

4. Last Now the tiny particles inside the piece of iron are

_____

What is a magnetic field?

When you pull or push something, you have to touch it. A magnet can pull or push without touching. How?

Every magnet has a magnetic field around it. A **magnetic field** is the area around a magnet where it can push or pull another magnet.

Look at the magnetic field traced by iron filings. If you move another magnet into this magnetic field, the two magnets will:

- attract if opposite poles are facing each other
- repel if like poles are facing each other.

The magnetic field is strongest at the poles. Farther away from the poles, the ability to attract or repel becomes weaker and weaker.

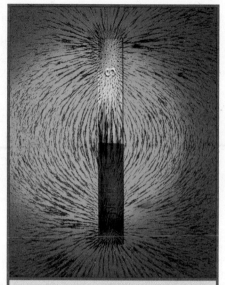

These tiny pieces of iron are on a glass plate held over a magnet. When the plate is shaken, the iron pieces trace the magnetic field around the magnet.

 **Quick Check**

Correct each of these *false* sentences.

5. You become positively charged when you walk across a rug. _____

_____

_____

6. You feel a shock when negative particles move from the doorknob

to your hand. _____

_____

What is a compass?

Earth is a giant magnet. Part of the inside of the Earth is made up of melted iron. This iron sets up a magnetic field around Earth.

The north pole of Earth's magnetic field is located near the geographic North Pole. Earth's magnetic south pole is located near the geographic South Pole.

A **compass** is a tool that gives directions. It is made up of a free-spinning magnetic needle that lines up with Earth's magnetic field. It points to the magnetic north pole.

Because a compass needle points north, the compass can be used to find all the other directions as well.

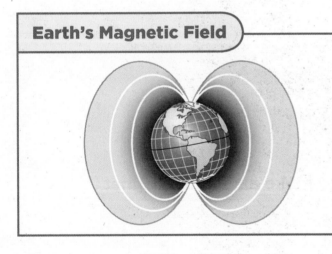

Earth's Magnetic Field

Reading Diagrams

Earth's magnetic field is strongest at the point where the field lines come together, at the north and south magnetic poles.

✔ Quick Check

In each row cross out the word (or words) that does (do) not belong.

7. magnetic field   attract   like poles   repel

8. north   equator   compass   south

LOG ON e-Review Summaries and quizzes online @ **www.macmillanmh.com**

What is an electromagnet?

When an electric current flows through a wire, it sets up a magnetic field around the wire. The field is stronger if you wind the wire into a coil.

Just add one more item, an iron rod (or nail), and you can make an electromagnet. An **electromagnet** is a magnet made when an electric current flows through a coil of wire wrapped around an iron rod. When current flows, the iron rod acts like a magnet. Its two ends become north and south poles.

To make current flow through the coiled wire, attach the ends of the wire to a battery.

 **Quick Check**

Complete the diagram to tell how to make an electromagnet.

9. First Wind a wire into a _____ .

10. Next Wrap the _____ .

11. Last Attach the ends of _____ .

How are electromagnets used?

Electromagnets are often more useful than permanent magnets because:

- you can turn them on and off by switching the current on and off
- you can make them stronger by increasing the current and/or the coils of wire.

Electromagnets are used in many things people use everyday, including:

- doorbells
- motors that run hobby trains and cars
- electric guitars.

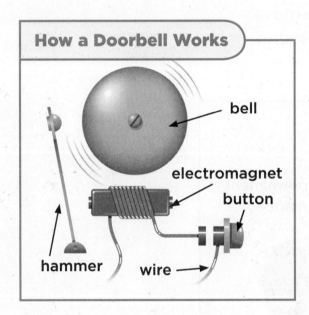

How a Doorbell Works

bell

electromagnet

button

hammer   wire

◀ **When you push the button, you switch the current on. The electromagnet pulls a hammer to strike a bell.**

✔ Quick Check

12. To turn on an electromagnet, all you have to do is _____

_____

13. One way to make an electromagnet stronger is to _____

_____

How does a loudspeaker work?

Electromagnets are used in loudspeakers. A **loudspeaker** is a device that changes electrical energy into sound. Loudspeakers produce sound in radios, stereos, televisions, and headphones.

Inside the loudspeaker, an electromagnet is attached to a diaphragm (DIGH•uh•fram). The *diaphragm* is a cup-like surface that can make sound when:

- a current flows through an electromagnet inside the loudspeaker
- the electromagnet is pushed and pulled by a permanent magnet
- at the same time, the diaphragm also moves back and forth (vibrates) and makes sound.

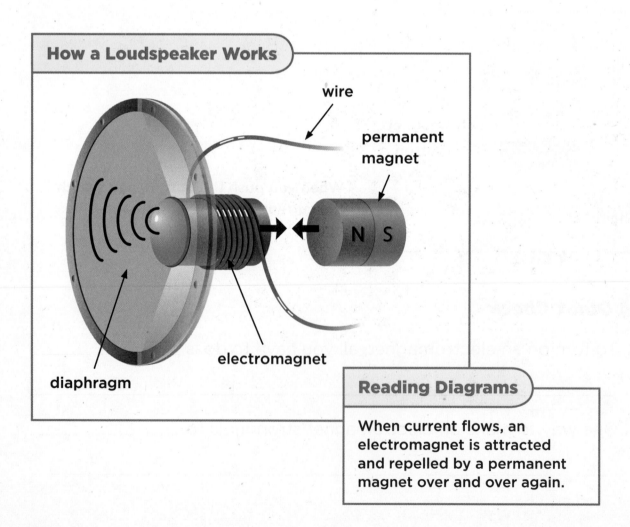

How a Loudspeaker Works

wire

permanent magnet

N S

electromagnet

diaphragm

Reading Diagrams

When current flows, an electromagnet is attracted and repelled by a permanent magnet over and over again.

Telephones

Telephones use electromagnets. A telephone receiver is a tiny loudspeaker. When someone calls you:

- the person speaks into a mouthpiece. The mouthpiece is often a microphone (MIGH•kruh•fohn). A **microphone** uses a magnet to change sound into electric signals
- the signals travel to your receiver
- your receiver uses an electromagnet just as any loudspeaker does—to change the signals into sound.

The Parts of a Receiver

loudspeaker

microphone

Reading Diagrams

The labels identify the two parts of a telephone used for peaking and listening.

 **Quick Check**

Match the object with its description.

14. ____ loudspeaker   **a.** changes sound into electric signals

15. ____ microphone   **b.** vibrating part of microphones and loudspeakers

16. ____ diaphragm

     c. changes electric signals into sound

LOG ON e-Review Summaries and quizzes online @ **www.macmillanmh.com**

What is an electric motor?

Just about any electrical device that has moving parts inside uses an electric motor. An electric **motor** changes electrical energy into motion.

Electric motors operate:

- air conditioners
- refrigerators
- electric toys, such as trains and cars
- power tools.

A simple electric motor has several parts:

- a source of power—such as a battery or a plug
- a permanent magnet
- a loop of wire that can spin
- a motor shaft—a rod that can spin and move

An electric motor in this toy car changes electric energy into the spinning motion of the wheels. ▶

Here is how a motor works:

1. An electric current runs through the wire loop, making a magnetic field around the coil.

2. The permanent magnet then pushes and pulls on the wire loop, making the loop spin.

3. The spinning wire loop spins the shaft.

4. The shaft, in turn, spins a wheel or gear.

In larger motors, the loop of wire is a coil of wire. The coil is wound hundreds of times around an iron tube. This makes a very strong electromagnet for moving heavy objects or making things move very fast.

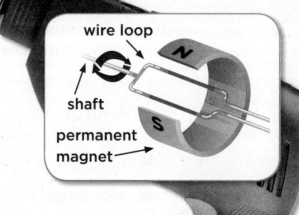

wire loop

shaft

permanent magnet

N

S

Reading Diagrams

An electric motor in this power drill changes electric energy into the spinning motion of the drill.

 Quick Check

Tell if each sentence is *true* or *false*. If *false*, correct the sentence.

17. Electric motors use motion to produce electrical energy.

_____

18. In a motor, a magnetic field is made around the wire coil.

_____

19. In a motor, the spinning wire loop spins the permanent magnet.

_____

What is a generator?

Almost all of our electrical energy is produced by generators (JEH•nuh•ray•turz). A **generator** changes motion into electrical energy. That is exactly the opposite of what a motor does.

Here's how a generator works:

1. Wind, flowing water, or steam is used to spin a *turbine* (TER•bin). A turbine is a part that looks like a pinwheel or an electric fan.

2. The turbine is connected to a wire loop. The spinning turbine turns the wire loop between the poles of a permanent magnet.

3. The magnet is surrounded by a magnetic field. Current flows through the wire loop as the loop moves through the magnetic field.

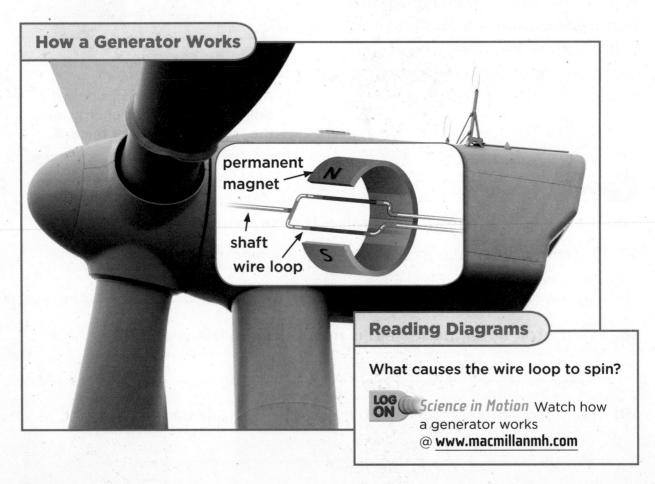

How a Generator Works

permanent magnet

N

shaft

wire loop

S

Reading Diagrams

What causes the wire loop to spin?

LOG ON *Science in Motion* Watch how a generator works @ **www.macmillanmh.com**

One way generators can work is by making a coil of wire spin inside a magnetic field. Another way generators can work is just the opposite. Make a magnetic spin inside of a coil of wire.

For example, to make this hand-made model work:

1. Spin the nail. The magnets stuck to the clay spin inside the coil of wire.

2. Current will flow through the coil of wire.

3. The current sets up a magnetic field around the compass. The magnetic field causes the compass needle to move. When you see the needle move, you know current is flowing.

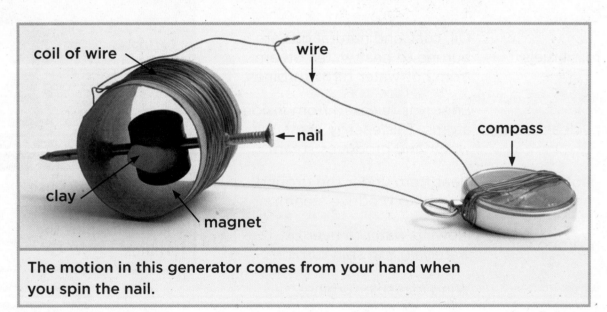

The motion in this generator comes from your hand when you spin the nail.

✔ Quick Check

Tell which of these steps happens first, second, and third. Label them *1*, *2*, and *3*.

20. _____ As the wire loop spins inside a magnetic field, current flows through the wire.

21. _____ The spinning turbine, in turn, causes a wire loop to spin.

22. _____ Wind or flowing water make a turbine spin.

What are sources of electrical energy?

A generator works because energy of motion is needed to make the turbine spin. Where does that energy of motion come from?

The word *source* (SAWRS) is used to describe where something comes from. Generators have several sources of energy.

Wind can spin a turbine without the need for heating water and producing steam.

Source of Energy	How It Is Used in a Generator
fossil fuels	Oil, coal, and natural gas are burned to heat water. Steam from hot water turns turbines.
nuclear energy	Energy is released from inside atoms. This energy heats water and produces steam.
geothermal energy	Heat from under the ground is used to produce steam.
hydropower	Flowing water (a river or waterfall) can spin turbines.
wind	Wind can spin turbines.

Many generators use heat to produce steam. The steam spins the turbines.

✔ Quick Check

23. Which sources of energy can spin a turbine without making steam?

_____

_____

What kinds of electric current are there?

The electric current that most generators make is an alternating current (AC). An **alternating current** flows in one direction and then in the opposite direction. Electrical charges flow back and forth, over and over again.

Alternating current is available in electrical wall outlets. You use alternating current when you plug in an electric device and turn it on.

When you use a battery, you are using direct current (DC). A **direct current** is an electric current that flows in just one direction.

Many computers need direct current. Yet you plug them into an outlet. These computers have a part inside that changes alternating current from the outlet into direct current.

The electric current from a wall outlet in your home is alternating current.

Quick Check

Summarize what you learned on this page by filling the diagram.

| 24. _____ | 25. _____ |

Summary

There are two kinds of electric current

LOG ON e**-Review** Summaries and quizzes online @ www.macmillanmh.com

Magnetism

Choose the letter of the best answer.

1. The area around a magnet where it can push or pull another magnet is a(n)

   a. magnetic field

   b. compass

   c. pole

   d. electric current

2. A magnet that is made when an electric current flows through a coiled wire around an iron rod is a(n)

   a. permanent magnet

   b. alternating magnet

   c. pole

   d. electromagnet

3. Electrical energy is changed into sound by a(n)

   a. generator

   b. microphone

   c. loudspeaker

   d. motor

4. Electrical current that flows in one direction and then in the opposite direction, back and forth, is a(n)

   a. direct current

   b. alternating current

   c. parallel

   d. closed

5. Electrical current that flows in just one direction is a(n)

   a. direct current

   b. alternating current

   c. parallel

   d. closed

6. Loudspeakers, microphones, and doorbells all work by using a(n)

   a. motor

   b. generator

   c. electromagnet

   d. turbine

Fill in each blank with a letter to spell out the answer.

1. Any object that pulls (or attracts) certain metal objects is

a(n) __ __ __ __ __ __.
<u> </u> <u> </u> <u> </u> <u> </u> <u>10</u> <u>11</u>

2. The part of a magnet where the ability to push or pull is the

strongest is a(n) __ __ __ __.
<u> </u> <u>2</u> <u>1</u> <u> </u>

3. A tool that shows directions by letting a needle line up with Earth's

magnetic field is a(n) __ __ __ __ __ __ __.
<u> </u> <u> </u> <u>8</u> <u> </u> <u>9</u> <u> </u> <u> </u>

4. Electrical energy is changed into energy of motion

by a(n) __ __ __ __ __.
<u> </u> <u>5</u> <u>7</u> <u> </u> <u> </u>

5. Sound is changed electric signals by a(n)

__ __ __ __ __ __ __ __ __ __.
<u> </u> <u>4</u> <u> </u> <u> </u> <u> </u> <u> </u> <u> </u> <u>3</u> <u> </u> <u> </u>

6. Energy of motion is changed into electrical energy by a(n)

__ __ __ __ __ __ __ __ __.
<u>12</u> <u> </u> <u> </u> <u> </u> <u>13</u> <u> </u> <u>6</u> <u> </u> <u> </u>

Use the letters in the numbered blanks to answer a question.

What do you get when you use a battery, a coil of wire, and an iron bar?

__ __ __ __ __ __ __ __ __ __ __ __ __
1 2 3 4 5 6 7 8 9 10 11 12 13